FLOW RIVER

Book 3 in the Saul Trader Series

by Keith Harris

The river flows
It flows to the sea
Wherever that river goes
That's where I want to be

Flow, river flow
Let your waters wash down
Take me from this road
To some other town

The Byrds - Ballad of Easy Rider

'Never let the truth get in the way of a good story,' Mark *Twain*

ACKNOWLEDGMENTS

Thank you to everyone who accompanied me on these trips. I consider myself lucky to have known such a lot of colourful characters.
I have tried to describe everyone accurately and portray them in a true but entertaining way. I sincerely hope I have not offended anyone but if so I apologise unreservedly.

Finally, a big thanks to Allen Maslen, who has guided me through the sometimes painful process of getting these books published.

CONTENTS

CONTENTS

Chapter 1   Inundation

I had left my barge, Saul Trader, safely moored at Laroche-Migennes, on the River Yonne alongside several other barges at the yard that was run by Joe Parfitt, in October 2008.

I was in the habit of abandoning the English winter for Thailand, and it was while I was there, basking in shorts and flip flops and 30° of heat that one evening in the middle of February I got an Email from Joe in Migennes which totally knocked me for six.

The temperature in Migennes had dropped as low as minus 15°C, something I found impossible to imagine, immersed as I was in 24 hour tropical heat. The valve on the engine fresh water intake on Saul Trader had apparently frozen and split and the boat had flooded and nearly sunk. My heart sunk similarly when I read this terrible news, and it took me a while to put it all into some sort of perspective. I called Joe to get the full story and he told me that it was thanks to the quick action of one of the girls who worked in the yard, Sarah, who had been working on the boat alongside, that the outcome wasn't a lot more serious. She had noticed something was wrong, and that Saul Trader had developed a list, and immediately called the Pompiers.

The result was a very large insurance payout which rather put paid to any thoughts of no-claim discount for the rest of my life! I got the distressing news by Email. I was pretty distraught, not helped by the fact that I was so far away and utterly helpless, which didn't exactly give me a lot of comfort. I lay awake trying to picture the mess and at one point I think I actually thought I was going to breakdown. Joe assured me he had everything in hand and there was little point in returning as there was nothing I would be able do at that stage.

Joe and his staff did everything they possibly could to minimise the damage and he gradually compiled a list of everything that he felt would need to be replaced. I notified the insurance company through my broker and was told to make a comprehensive list of the likely cost. They also told me that they would be sending out their loss adjuster, a marine surveyor, before agreeing to any claim. This was another stressful time. Would they try to wriggle out of it by maintaining that the damage had resulted from a faulty valve? Initially they did try to suggest that the valve hadn't been fully closed but thanks to Joe this theory was dismissed and they conceded that there was a genuine bona fide claim. The only exception to this, due to a clause buried somewhere in the small print of the policy, was anything mechanical. Fortunately the engine and generator were saved - no small thanks due to the speedy response by the Pompiers. At one point the water in the saloon was over a foot deep. All in all it didn't make for a very relaxing couple of months in the Far East, 6000 miles away.

When I got back in the UK in the April, I started to go through a list of the items that would we would be claiming for - all the bedding, mattresses, sheets and duvets, the fridge, inverter and Webasto boiler, CDs and books and canal guides and charts, electrical sockets, Bose Ipod dock and some other electrical accessories that had suffered mainly from damp.

We ventured to Migennes in the Spring with heavy hearts and Transit van. I had bought four new mattresses and all the other bedding items that had been ruined, which we loaded into the van along with several boxes of books. I took my friend Jerry Pawlak along with me - "that Rambo bloke" as Scragg had christened him some years earlier , a big strong and practical mate with the strength to get the heavier stuff on to the boat. We really didn't know what to expect but feared the worst. What we found was pretty devastating but could have been a lot worse. The boat was certainly not habitable and we had to stay in a small chambres d'hote a few miles away on the banks of the Yonne for three days before we had the boat aired out sufficiently to be able to move back aboard. Amazingly the carpets had dried out and looked almost as new (they had needed cleaning, to be honest!), and the woodwork showed no signs of the inundation - another testimony to the quality of the work and the materials used by RWD, the boat's builder.

The engine and generator had survived virtually unscathed apart from the oil cooler that Joe had replaced, but unfortunately some of the electrics could not be saved. The inverter was ruined and although Joe thought the Webasto boiler that was situated on the engine room floor would also need replacing, in fact it started up at the first try and has performed without a problem ever since. This accelerated the drying out process and meant that within a few days the boat had regained some of its old feel. Another absolutely essential item that was irrepairable was the Bose Ipod dock, something I could definitely not live without, as combined with my iPod it had become the main source of entertainment on board. The soft furnishings had suffered mainly from damp but with a bit of warmth from the spring sunshine were soon restored to normality. There were also half a dozen large boxes full of soggy books with their pages welded together that had to be discarded. Amongst them were two of the formative books on European Waterways, "Slow Boat Through France", and "Slow Boat Through Germany", by the English author Hugh McKnight. By a strange twist of fate I was in Thailand at an auction the following year when I noticed a pile of books looking somewhat forlorn on the top of a rattan chest of drawers. On closer inspection I saw that they were all books about canals - European canals. There were about a dozen of them altogether, all in good condition, and in the middle of the pile, the two Hugh McKnight volumes that I had lost - amazingly, both signed by the author. They had already been through the auction but hadn't sold, (not a lot of call for books on European Canals in Thailand), and after a few minutes negotiation with the boss, I bought them, all twelve of them, for 500 Baht, which at the time equated to about £10.

I had always marvelled at how quickly Saul Trader returned to normal within a couple of days of our return after six months of winter hibernation and it was the same now. After three or four days of concentrated cleaning and drying we were almost ready to set sail again. Saul Trader had shrugged off the experience almost as though nothing untoward had happened.

7

While we were there another of Jerry's talents were put to good use. Joe had a large steel delivery from Poland. The lorry driver was having difficulty understanding Joe's instructions. By chance we had someone with us fluent in Polish. Jerry's parents were Polish refugees and he had picked up the language at an early age from his mother, which meant that he was able to act as interpreter which greatly helped the operation. He even managed to give the driver directions to get him back on to the autoroute after he had unloaded his truck.

We returned to England a few days later feeling quite a lot better. The total claim came to over £20,000 and to their credit, the insurance company, Navigators & General, paid out promptly in full without any argument.

Owing to the trauma and uncertainty caused by all this over the past few months, I hadn't made any definite plans for the summer. I had originally intended to go to Paris for a DBA rally in the Canal Saint-Martin, a route that led off from the Arenal through the backwaters of the city, but unfortunately this had to be abandoned due to the circumstances.

Joe, as president of the Friends of the Nivernais Society, was organising a rally in conjunction with the Kennet & Avon Society, which was to take place at Vincelles a few months later. He obviously wanted to attract as many boats as possible and I thought the least we could do by way of appreciation for his help, was to give him some support. Saul Trader needed a fresh work-up trial to test the newly installed equipment so it was decided to head for the rally, which was scheduled for the middle of July, by a circular route, via the Canals, Loing, Briare and Loire, in the opposite direction that we'd taken a few years ago, then south to Decize and back north on the Nivernais to Vincelles. I am definitely not one for rallies, although I had been looking forward to Paris, but this would be a good alternative - and Rob, who was a long-standing friend of Joe's, was also going with his boat, the "Pisgah".

I went back to Migennes in the middle of June with a boot full of new books that I had bought with some of the insurance money. There were all the Cartes Guides and various canal books that I had been able to find via the Internet and I think I just about managed to replace all those that had been water-damaged. Rob had been talking about a music festival that was held each year at Samois sur Seine, a few kilometres from Fontainbleu. It was the place where the king of Gypsy jazz guitar, Django Reinhardt, had retired to in 1951, and the festival was a celebration of his life and work. I knew nothing about him at all but the idea of a bit of jazz appealed so we decided to take the boats. It would mean just a short half-day diversion from St Mammés, which we would be passing anyway en route to the Canal de Loing.

While we were in Migennes, my old friend Fergus Shalloo, who lived next door to the Cape of Good Hope in Warwick, turned up on his way to Spain and stayed for a couple of days. He had sold his boat, the Polynomial, and bought himself a strange little motorhome. I think it was a Mazda Bongo, or something like that, and Ferg set out to explore the World in it. I don't know why but it reminded me of one of those invalid cars where the driver sits up very high and looks as though his head would come out through the top. It could have been a secondhand Popemobile, but Ferg was as pleased as Punch with it. He bumped and swayed over the pot-holes into the yard with a cheeky smile, spotted the boat, and reversed - straight into one of those one-man portaloos. It was only a gentle nudge but it sent the little cubicle rocking from side to side for several seconds before coming to rest.

When he emerged from the car grinning from ear to ear I told him that the occupant had been suffering from constipation for a week and he had just provided an instant cure.

He had managed to achieve in two seconds flat what Ex-Lax gaurantees to do in 24 hours!

Ferg had a bit of history as far as moveable homes are concerned. He once bought a small caravan and attached it to his Vauxhall Cavalier outside the Cape to go for a trial run. He stopped at the junction with Cape Road and looked in his rear-view mirror, only to see the caravan gathering speed backwards down the slope towards the canal. According to a couple of eye-witnesses, he leapt out of the car and chased after the escaping caravan, just managing, with the help of a few of the regulars, to arrest its progress seconds before it became a floating home. Apparently he had forgotten to take the rubber cover off the tow-hitch before connecting the caravan to the car - something that could have happened to any Irishman!

Ferg stayed for a couple of days. He turned down my offer of a berth, instead preferring to sleep inside the roof compartment of the Bongo, although he always appeared in the morning just as the bacon was sizzling in the pan. That evening we ate on deck with Rob and his girlfriend, Wendy, and Ferg had us in stitches with tales of the latest goings-on around the Cape of Good Hope. Not that Cape of Good Hope - he hadn't travelled that far in the Bongo, but the waterside canal pub beside the Cape Locks in Warwick. He told us about an old chap called Donald who moored on a dilapidated boat opposite the pub and who would come into the pub for a few pints every lunchtime, on the dot of one o'clock.

One day his false teeth broke and Paul, the Landlord, attempted a repair. He told Donald to hold the broken set together while he poured on some Superglue - well half a tube of the stuff to be exact, which of course had the effect of bonding his fingers and hands to the teeth. Unable to go too long without a sip of beer, Donald had then picked up his jug to take a drink. This caused the handle to become inexorably stuck to the assemblage so that each time Donald lifted his hand to take a drink, the teeth and both his hands rose simultaneously with the glass. Unfortunately the teeth got in the way of any contact with his mouth, which resulted in much hilarity in the pub as Donald contorted his head and neck in a vain attempt to get some of the beer down his throat. Eventually he had to resort to tipping the glass above his head which meant that most of the beer bypassed his mouth altogether and ended up running over his head and down the back of his neck. Just how all of this was resolved Ferg couldn't say, as he, along with several others, had needed to visit the loo in a bit of a hurry, when the excessive laughter had almost caused a damp accident in the groin area!

Oh! The weather was cold and the engine was old,
And the butty boat started to leak,
And we hit Smethwick pier 'cos me mate couldn't steer
And we didn't get washed for a week!

Our womenfolk brave gave us a great wave
As we started that journey historic,
But we ran out of soap at the Cape of Good Hope,
That's the name of the boozer at Warwick.
From; The 'Orrible Trip by David Blagrove

By this time Ferg was in full swing.
"To long a cut story short," he began, before spending the next half an hour telling us all about his encounter with a particularly alien toll booth on the Autoroute. The French are rather less than accommodating in this regard for the beleaguered British driver, who sits on the opposite side of the vehicle to his French counterpart, somewhat inconsiderately siting the ticket dispensers on the "wrong" side of the British car.
Ferg, arriving at his first meeting with one of these space stations, and not really having much idea about the procedures required, slowed down to watch the vehicle in front glide slowly towards the opening, and just at the point of near contact with the barrier, saw it swing into the air, obligingly allowing the Renault Megane to speed through into the daylight. No problem then, thinks Ferg, and follows him into the lane. He slowed down just as he had seen the Frenchman - and nothing happened. The barrier stayed resolutely in place, with a bewildered Ferg looking like a horse left at the starting gate at Aintree. He looked around for inspiration but all he saw was a queue of cars piling up behind. He thought about charging the barrier. He couldn't understand what had gone wrong.
A Frenchman from the car behind appeared at his window and Ferg pushed the button to open it only to realise that that particular button operated the rear window. Panic and consternation set in until he found the correct winder. Then all

11

became clear - clear as mud as the Frenchman proceeded to tell him exactly where he was going wrong..

"Avez-vous une carte de péage Sanef? Si vous ne l'avez pas vous êtes dans la mauvaise voie. Vous devriez utiliser une des autres voies et les prendre un ticket.

Maintenant, vous causez un gros problème parce que toutes les voitures derrière devront se déplacer de sorte que vous pouvez inverser sortir et aller à la bonne voie.

Comprenez vous?

All this delivered in the way that Frenchmen always do when speaking to foreigners - at ninety miles an hour. Now needless to say, Ferg's command of French was on a par with his knowledge of Uzbekistani.

"Would you be able to speak a little slower, please", he suggested.

At last, with elaborate use of hand signals accompanied by a cacophony of hoots from the frustrated motorists queueing up behind, a vague notion of the message was conveyed. Ferg had to reverse back out of the lane that was reserved for people who had an electronic tag affixed to their vehicle which allowed them free passage, the toll being charged automatically to their Bank account. The whole idea of this was that the regular in- the- know travellers, could pass through the Péages with a minimum of delay. That is until a bloody stupid Irishman in a Bongo fouled up the entire network. Not only did Ferg not have one of these magical devices, I'm not sure he even had a bank account.

At this point a Gendarme appeared and Ferg had visions of camping in the Bongo within the confines of a Police compound.

"Why are you here?" enquired the policeman, and Ferg had to admit that the same thought had occurred to him.

Eventually, with a good deal of effing and blinding (in French of course) the queue, which now numbered some dozen or more cars, was herded backwards to allow the Bongo to make its shameful retreat. Ferg smiled nervously as he circled the mob and finally managed to find another lane. The next problem was what to do next. The barrier once again stayed firmly closed. Ferg looked around and then he saw it. A bright yellow machine, out of which poked a cheekily inviting looking ticket.

"Of course, of course".

Memories of his last trip to France some ten years earlier came flooding back and it dawned on him that he needed to take the ticket. This is where the awkwardness of the French psyche and their determination to make everything as difficult as possible for the Irish becomes acutely apparent. The bloody thing was of course on the wrong side of the Bongo - and the Bongo was too wide for Ferg to reach across. He did try. Having first pressed the wrong button again and opened the rear window, Ferg then stretched himself across the passenger seat and attempted to pull out the ticket - and he very nearly made it.

He managed to get his head and shoulders through the window and in fact he was only a few inches from success when he overbalanced and tipped himself on to his arse off the seat and into the footwell. Having recovered his position, if not his composure, and performed a double-jointed manoeuvre to get himself back in the driver's seat, he made a bold and determined decision. Having become aware of a deafening noise, he looked behind to see at least another hundred cars lined up behind him. Some had even got out of their vehicles and were waving at him in a not altogether friendly way, and one or two were taking pictures of him on their cell phones.

Well - he'd show them that the Irish were not to be defeated by some petit masochistic twat whose boring life was only made bearable by doing everything possible to make life awkward and piss off even the most even tempered Irishman. Sod 'em. He would get out of the Bongo and walk to the bloody machine. That would show 'em!

So he sauntered cockily round to the haughty-looking yellow robot and nonchalantly plucked the ticket from its mouth. Then as he then turned around his arm brushed the wing mirror of the Bongo as he passed, which caused the ticket to become detached from his grasp, dance to and fro in the breeze, and then swoop gently downward before disappearing underneath the car. By this time, of course, the barrier and risen, and the light glowed green, impatiently awaiting the

Bongo to make its exit. As he got down on hands and knees to retrieve the errant piece of card from underneath the car, Ferg couldn't help but notice that the number of waiting cars had now increased by at least another hundred and one of the drivers had the audacity to be walking towards him, video-ing the whole debacle on his bloody phone.

At last he got back into the Bongo, armed with the ticket, and sped off into the sunset - but not before giving the watching crowd a triumphant two-fingered salute. You think you can beat Paddy - well you've got another think coming, Pierre!

It was several days later that Ferg admitted to us that he had made up most of the story - well maybe not all of it, I think he had embellished it a bit. He had in fact tried to drive through the automatic barrier, and one or two cars had needed to reverse out of his way so that he could correct his error, and his excuse was that he had made up the whole story to relieve the boredom of the autoroute as he lumbered along for mile after mile with the Bongo flat out doing 62 and a half miles an hour.

It made for some good entertainment nevertheless, as we could all picture him doing exactly what he had described. After all, you should never let the truth spoil a good story. That reminded Rob of another old story about an Irishman stopped at a breathalyser checkpoint.

"Would you blow into this bag please sir," said the copper.

Paddy produces an official-looking card from his wallet that says that owing to a medical condition he should not be subjected to anything that might aggravate his breathing.

"OK," says Mr Plod, "we'll go to the station where you will have to undergo a blood test."

Paddy then reaches in his inside pocket and brings out another card which says that he is a haemophiliac with a rare blood disorder and must not be subjected to anything that might cause him to lose blood.

"Right then," says the policeman, not to be outdone, "Down to the station then - you'll have to do a urine test."

Then out comes another card from his trouser pocket.

"Don't take the piss out of Paddy".

Chapter 2 ... Underway at Last

We set off for the Seine and the jazz festival in beautiful mid-summer weather. Rob and Wendy, and Mike and Sue from Norfolk who had driven down to join me on Saul Trader.

I had known them from my days at sea with P&O when I sailed on the good ship Pando Head with Mike, who in those days was the third mate. Our regular runs were out from the UK via the Cape of Good Hope (the Suez Canal was still closed to shipping in those days), for a month loading and unloading around the Far East - Penang, Port Swettenham, Singapore, Hong Kong, Manila, Yokohama, Kobe and Kaoishung, then a month back to the UK followed by a three or four week "coastal" around such Channel ports as Rotterdam, Antwerp and Hamburg and Hull.

The Pando Head was originally called the Surat, like the rest of the general cargo fleet that bore wonderfully evocative names with Far East connotations - the Ballarat, Bendigo, Comorin, Coromandel, Cannanore, Patonga, and Sunda, but in their wisdom P&O had decided to re-name them all with the Pando suffix. The intention was to streamline the fleet overnight and turn them from glorified trampers into modern fast cargo liners. Unfortunately it didn't work as they could still only manage about 14 knots flat out and owing to their manually operated hatches could not load or unload in the rain. Mike kept the midnight (or as he called it, the Oh Christ double o to 0400 watch and I would often join him on the bridge for a few hours for a chat and a cup of cocoa.

Yes I know - "It was on the bridge at midnight etc etc!"

I was studying for my Yachtmasters Exam by correspondence course at the time which was then under the jurisdiction of the Board of Trade. Apart from navigation and meteorology papers, there were practical tests in Morse code and Semaphore signalling so these exercises were not just good fun, but also helped me with the course. We would flash up passing ships on the Aldis Lamp, usually asking "What ship -

where bound." Sometimes we could get no response at all and assumed that everyone on the bridge must be asleep, but at other times we would get an immediate reply.

"Port Moresby - Singapore bound Liverpool."

This would invariably inspire me, on instruction from Mike, to signal back "VHF" and we would then have a brief conversation, usually involving telephone numbers for nurses homes or teacher training colleges in the places we were heading for, that were always good for a party. There was a little book kept on the bridge entitled "Ships that Pass in the Night" where details of these encounters would be duly logged. I treasured those nights, especially in the humid stillness of the Tropics, when Mike and I would put the World to rights and dream of so many things we were going to do when we left the sea. It all seemed so simple then and needless to say none of them actually ever got off the ground, but they were fun while they lasted.

I had made up a rough hammock from a couple of canvas laundry bags which I would sling up on deck while we were in the Tropics. One of Mike's jobs on the 12 to 4 was to 'blow the tubes.' The Pando Head (ex Surat) ran on FFO - furnace fuel oil, which caused quite a bit of clag to accumulate, and this had to be periodically blown out of the funnel. Every now and then Mike would get a message from the engine-room to "Blow Tubes." When he knew I was sleeping on the deck he would alter course so that the wind was blowing directly over my makeshift bed as he blew the shit out so that some mornings I would wake up covered in great flakes of black soot.

My Goanese cabin boy, Lino, bringing my morning cup of tea up to the deck , once exclaimed,

"What fashion this sahib? You looking same me, isn't it!"

On reflection, we were probably helping to hasten the advent of global warming!

Another little party piece of mine was re-enacted on each trip as we sailed back to England. At about the time that we were crossing the Equator, one of my jobs was to do a stock take of the ship's freezers. This would take me about three hours and meant dressing up in submarine jumper, duffle coat and hood, woolly socks, gloves and sea boots as protection from the sub-

16

zero temperatures. When I finished the job I would make a point of parading up and down the main deck, where the crew were sunning themselves in the tropical heat, dressed like an Eskimo, a little scenario that never failed to get a laugh.

The first night after leaving Migennes we moored at Joigny alongside the road, and ate in a restaurant that Rob knew. We shared the paella for four which could just as well have fed eight!

A lot of the locks on the River Yonne were constructed with sloping sides in order to provide extra strength in the walls, and the next day we had a minor incident when Pisgah got caught on an obstruction in the sloping wall and finished up at a rather alarming angle. The lock-keeper was a young female student who had disappeared into her office and was completely unaware of what was happening. She later maintained that there was no way of stopping the lock from emptying, something I found hard to believe, as all locks are fitted with an emergency stop button. Luckily the lock was near to the bottom of its fall or the outcome could have been a lot more serious. We were tied on to a floating pontoon and the eclusiere let us out of the lock before slowly filling it enough to re-float Pisgah.

Pisgah in trouble in the slope-sided lock

....and happier times with Mike and Sue at the BBQ

Back at Moret sur Loing, we tied alongside the 'Peke' which was owned by another former working narrowboater, known only by the pseudonym of "Angry", given to him back in the 1970's by Nick Hill. Nicholas and his wife Judy were "enjoying", if that's the word, a week's boating with their old friends. I got the impression that they had been waiting for the opportunity to open their hearts into a sympathetic ear. They'd been together for about a week and I quickly discovered that this was about six days too long.

"They've eaten us out of everything" moaned Angry, "a whole bloody pound of butter they've got through - in a bloody week."

"He's bloody hopeless," Nick complained, "ne, ne, never wants to go anywhere. We didn't s,s,s,set off till 1.00 o'clock yesterday. Bloody ho, ho, hopeless." We left them to their holiday bliss and as we had a couple of days spare, decided to go off for a short cruise on the canal. Nick insisted on accompanying us through the lock, ranting continually about "bloody useless Angry."

We headed for a place that Rob knew at Beaumoulin Lock on the Canal de Loing for a barbecue. After a pleasant and peaceful trip we reached the spot where we were to tie up in a convenient lay-by. Sod's law then raised its ugly head again as no less than four loaded peniches passed us in the space of thirty minutes as we were trying to get alongside the bank.

There was a small grass area beside the canal and we soon had the barbecue lit up, the charcoal glowing and the steaks sizzling, the beer opened and a bit of music from the boat - parfait.

The Django Reinhardt festival was interesting. Jo Parfitt came up from Migennes with his Dutch partner Door, or Do, but call her Dorothea at your peril, and stayed in the back cabin, and the weather stayed fine and warm. We moored in the narrow by-pass stream and Rob, true to form, managed to cock-up his approach, having been invited by the large Dutch owner of an immaculate Tjalk to breast up to him. After much shoving and swearing and luckily no scraped varnish, Pisgah rested quietly alongside. We then went alongside Pisgah which was fine but meant having to clamber over the two boats to get ashore. A fourth vessel then arrived and tied outside us so we were now four boats deep. The wife of the new arrival got an enormous welcoming bollocking from Uit, the owner of the Tjalk, for walking on his flawless and obviously expensively painted deck in her stiletto heels.

The festival site was situated on a small island in the river with access via a narrow footbridge. This had obvious advantages for the organisers as everyone had to cross the bridge to get to the action, so unless you wanted to swim, you had to pay. There were several stages, with the main one having the luxury of a seated grandstand. I did find the music a bit repetitive - once you had sat through an hour and a half of gypsy jazz, the last thing you wanted was another hour and a half of gypsy jazz.

On the Sunday morning Rob and I decided to cycle along the river to Fontainbleu. Rob also had a fold-up bike but it was not exactly a Brompton by any stretch of the imagination. It was more like the fold-up bike equivalent of a Norman Nippy. It had the worrying habit of trying to fold itself up whilst in motion - until Rob realised that he hadn't bolted it up correctly. We had a quiet couple of beers and on the way back Rob had a slight contretemps with a lamp-post, when the bike decided to go round the opposite side of it to the one that Rob had selected. The result of this was a crumpled heap of Rob groaning in the gutter. Rob was 70 at the time and still skied every year with his son so the small matter of a couple of grazed knees and a broken arm was never going to deter him.

"You were lucky the ground broke your fall," I ventured, in an attempt at sympathy.

We were also joined by Terry - or 'Strimmer of the Yard' as he had come to be known.

Terry had cycled to Migennes from Kent, (although I think he cheated a bit on the Channel Crossing and came on the ferry), for the dubious pleasure of a few weeks' work at Jo's yard, where he had been let loose with the company strimmer. In a couple of weeks he had unearthed enough antique ironmongery and obsolete junk from the undergrowth to have supplied a complete Beaulieu Boatjumble. "Strimmer" was good with bikes and had a super-charged racing bicycle pump

20

that he used to inflate the tyres on the Brompton to unimaginable levels, giving at least an extra 10 kilometres an hour!

After the weekend we returned to St Mammés and the three of us spent the evening sitting on the stern of Pisgah with a box of Cabanet Sauvignon Rouge - 5 Euros from the Casino Supermarché, and a cheese plate. Rob kept us amused with a succession of old Yorkshire jokes.

"A bloke walks into a pub in Barnsley and there are three old boys in cloth caps sitting in the corner with halves of mild playing dominoes.

"Is there a B&Q in Barnsley?" the stranger enquires.

After a pause, one of the regulars looks over the top of his hand of dommies and replies

"No - just a "B".

Bloke with haemorrhoids goes into a chemist shop and asks.

"Hast thou any arse cream?"

"Aye lad, Magnum or Cornetto."

A Yorkshireman's dog dies and as it was a favourite pet he decides to have a gold statue made by a jeweller to remember the dog by.

Yorkshireman: "Can tha mek us a gold statue of yon dog?"

Jeweller: "Do you want it 18 carat?"

Yorkshireman: "No I want it chewin' a bone yer daft bugger!"

Rob then started reminiscing about the delights of Yorkshire and particularly his home city of Sheffield. He started to sing the chorus of a song that mourned the demise of the Sheffield steel industry,

"Going Down to Steelos, gonna meck a start."

Then someone, probably Strimmer, suggested naming all our favourite songs, and this then led to us acting out our own vino-inspired version of Desert Island Discs. Rob was chosen as the first special 'guest' and Strimmer did the Roy Plumley bit. I was IC music courtesy of the Ipod. We sat on the stern of Pisgah and nearly fell over the side laughing as Strimmer's questions got more ludicrous by the glass. The beauty of it was

21

that during the music bits we had time to re-fill our glasses, a highly conducive way to pass an evening.

"And so Rob, tell us just when your affair with Joan Collins began."

Just where Strimmer had managed to drag this unlikely theory from was anyone's guess, and something that not even Strimmer could say for sure.

"I'm sorry Rob, I haven't got 'I did it My Way' on my Ipod - or the theme from Postman bloody Pat."

Rob's musical tastes were a bit basic. His next request was for Harry Belafonte singing "Old Man River". I had six and a half thousand tunes on my Ipod but unfortunately none that Rob requested. I substituted with The Levellers and "The Boatman" hoping that nobody would notice.

'If I could choose the life I please I would be a boatman.'

"What the bloody hell is this crap?" Rob spat, "this isn't 'Arry."

No culture, these Yorkshire tykes - "still - not bad though", he was forced to concede.

The following day we spent recovering from the previous night's excesses and had a quiet meal on the quay at St Mammés with our old friend Gil, captain of the Peniche "Tigris", who still couldn't quite understand what all the hilarity of the previous night had been about. The next day we said our farewells to St Mammés, Gil and Pisgah, and headed back south on the Canal du Loing. Rob was going back to Migennes and we arranged to meet up again in a few weeks for the gathering at Vincelles. We had a pleasant and uneventful day, apart from being held up for 30 minutes at Ecluse 10 by an unnecessarily awkward lock-keeper, before spending the night at Bagneaux. Then, as we approached Montargis, our peace was somewhat rudely shattered as we passed beneath the Grand Larcy railway bridge. A group of bored local anarchists had decided to brighten up their pointless existence by emptying the railway of as much ballast as possible and hurling it at us! I suddenly realised how our Merchant sailors must have felt in the Atlantic as their ships were attacked with German artillery - huge rocks exploded in the water alongside, one bounced off the after deck and another crashed against the window.

"Weren't you lot on our bloody side" I shouted, but I don't think history had been one of their best subjects.

I fleetingly wished that Saul Trader had been fitted with a Bofor. We could have blown the bridge, and the assailants, into oblivion. I didn't even have a crossbow on board. Ferg once told me how he had warded off a bunch of delinquents in the middle of Birmingham.

"I quietly rested the crossbow onto the slide and gently pulled back the bolt," he said, "you should have seen the little bastards run."

I grabbed the first weapon that came to hand, and without thinking about the consequences, I took aim - and shot the nearest protagonist. There was no time to put the setting on to a fast shutter speed but nevertheless I managed to shoot him in full flow with an action shot on automatic focus, his right arm raised with an action any Pakistani bowler would have been proud of, clutching a lethal chunk of ballast above his shoulder and grinning menacingly.

"That'll teach you, you little bastard," I yelled, and it did, although not before he'd let fly with his ammunition which fortunately landed some 3 feet behind us with an almighty splash.

As soon as we were out of range I checked the damage. One of the wheelhouse windows had been marked with the sort of bullseye that you get when a stone thrown up by a truck hits your windscreen on the motorway, but luckily it hadn't penetrated. There was some damage on the aft deck which was not so bad and could be easily repaired with a rub down and a couple of coats of paint. The photograph had turned out very well, even though I had hardly had the time to take a proper aim. Furthermore, just around the next bend on the approach to Montargis, was the headquarters of the Gendarmerie and a conveniently adjacent mooring. Justice would be seen to be done. Two years hard labour breaking rocks on the Isle of Elba for railway ballast I thought would do the trick quite appropriately. The Gendarmes were sympathetic and apologised, without too much sincerity I thought, for the behaviour of their wayward youth, which was a very rare occurrence on their manor. The "Chef" took the sim card from the camera and asked for permission to take a copy. When he returned he showed me the blown up foolscap-size picture which I had to admit was rather good. The Chef smiled and said

"I know this boy very well. I will go to see his family today. Do not worry"

I hadn't any intention of worrying to be honest - well not much anyway. If anything I was disappointed that another theory had been shattered. We had spent eight years travelling the canals of France and nothing like this had ever happened before. All the young people we had come across had been polite and friendly and I was under the obviously false impression that this was down to the superior education system and the time-honoured family traditions and values that still seemed to be upheld in the land of freedom and brotherhood. True, I had heard rumours of barges being cut free from their moorings and of night-time thefts but these were surely isolated and exaggerated. The sport of hurling rocks at boaters, I had assumed, was strictly the preserve of the lawless English.

I thanked the Chef, gave him my mobile number, and was assured that he would let me know the outcome of his visit to the offender's parents. Whether he actually went to see them or not I never found out.

Imagine our shock then, when just two days later, we had another similar incident! Not rocks this time, but pea gravel shovelled by several pairs of feet from a footbridge just outside the town of Briare. The effect was similar to a hailstorm, with stones rather than balls of ice. The whole of the boat was covered with thousands of these tiny pebbbles. My first thought was that it was the work of the same gang, or their sympathisers, but I soon dismissed this as a bit of paranoid fantasy.

As soon as we had tied up on the quay at Briare, I set about clearing up the mess. There was no damage to the paint to speak of, but I couldn't just brush the stones off as this would have scratched and scoured the paintwork. I decided that the best way to remove them was with the hose, so I opened the deck wash valves and started the engine to engage the pump. The idea was working well and I had cleared the fore deck, when Mike came nonchalantly up to me and said.

"I think you'd better have a look in the engine room - it's filling up with water!"

Now Mike was used to dealing with mini crises. As third mate on the Pando Head he was also the designated medical officer and he had diligently applied himself to this role and avidly read "Teach Yourself Surgery" from cover to cover. Although as luck would have it, nothing too death-threatening happened during this time, there were occasions when Mike's knowledge of all things medical would be called into urgent action - like the time for example when Richard, the fourth engineer, was stung on the thigh by something tropical and potentially deadly. Mike coolly took Richard to the "surgery," an unused store-room, and inspected the damage.

"OK," said Mike with some authority, "an anti hysterical injection, that's what's needed," and with this produced a syringe with a 6 inch needle from his medical chest.

Now Richard, who was from Wigan, wasn't the brightest of engineers, or the bravest, but he was a simple and trusting soul.

"Are you sure, Mike?" he asked trembling a bit.

"Well - unless you want to risk getting gangrene in your leg and having to have it cut off," said Mike reassuringly. "Drop your trousers and I'll go and get the vaccine."

At this point Mike went around the ship and gathered anyone that was not otherwise engaged (which was probably most of them), to come and quietly watch the delicate operation.

Four heads peered around the door as Richard bent obediently over the bunk with his trousers and underpants dutifully dropped.

"Hold on," said Mike, "this will only hurt a bit."

Richard winced and Mike whacked him firmly on the arse with a rolled-up newspaper, causing much mirth and hilarity among the spectators.

"Aw Mike," groaned Richard, "I knew that's what you were going to do."

25

Another example of the exemplary calm under pressure shown by Mike came one night on a P&O ship of the line that I won't name for legal reasons. The evening's entertainment had come in the form of a frog-racing meeting, something that took place periodically at sea to relieve the boredom and relieve some members of the crew of their hard-earned wages. This particular night things had gone unusually well and the bar takings had soared. The Purser also had reason to be cheerful as he was assigned the job of dodgy bookie and had done rather well with his odds calculations.

The second engineer had theatrically removed his shirt at one point to put it on a race. The result of all this was that the off duty crew had all enjoyed a jolly good time but unfortunately some had conveniently forgotten that they had to go to work at midnight. However with true dedication the engine room watch had descended to their station in the lift as normal.

Mike was on the bridge and at 0200 decided to enquire whether they would be blowing tubes, which would require a reduction in engine speed, but for some reason he was unable to get any response on the voice tube to the engine room. After several failed attempts he decided to investigate, leaving the seacunny in charge of the wheel. Mike pressed the button and up came the engine room lift. The doors opened and there on the floor, dead to the world, lay the entire 12 to 4 engine room watch! Mike merely shook them awake, made sure they were capable of staying upright, closed the lift doors and sent them back down to their rightful place of work.

I have illustrated these examples purely to show just how efficiently and professionally Mike dealt with these unexpected occurrences. It was the same now that he had found the engine room on Saul Trader rapidly taking in water. I wished that I possessed the same qualities of composure but unfortunately I didn't and my immediate reaction went something like.

"Fucking hell what's happened now for Christ's sake."

The next thing I remember was standing in a foot of water trying to work out whether we had sprung a leak when the realisation dawned on me. A few days earlier I had emptied the stern bilge and I had obviously forgotten to close the valve. A similar thing had happened many years ago in Gloucester docks. On that occasion it had been the forward bilge and it had taken Darrell, the previous owner, to solve the problem.

Of course, idiot! When the deck wash valve was open it would take in water from the canal and pump it back out through the hose - that is provided that all the other bilge valves were closed. What was happening was that most of the water coming into the pump was siphoning back in to the bilge and gradually filling up the boat. An easy mistaker to maker. At least, I suppose, slightly forgivable under pressure. As soon as I had closed the deck wash intake valve the water level in the engine started to subside as the stern bilge valve did its job and soon conditions reverted to normal - well, as "normal" as they were ever likely to get.

The Briare harbourmaster, Bruno, arrived shortly afterwards, and when I explained what had happened, suggested calling the Police. From recent experience however, I told him not to bother.

The rest of the trip down to Decize passed peacefully without an airborne rock in sight. I wondered whether all the thugs had been put to work breaking up railway ballast but I had serious doubts. A more likely outcome was that they were safely back in school.

At Menetreol sur Sancerre we had to hover around for a bit as there were no vacant moorings until we were given permission to breast up with a nice little barge that was flying a pure un-defaced blue ensign. I thanked the skipper and gave him one of my best Sea Cadet salutes - up two three cut - but he didn't react, other than to give me a suspicious looking sideways glance. I don't know whether he was in fact a retired RN Admiral or whether he was flying the flag illegally as he disappeared below and never gave me a chance to talk. I think there may be one of the Royal Yacht clubs that does allow members to fly this but I'm not entirely sure. As far as I know it is still a beheading offence to fly one if you don't have the right. He may well have bought it at a boot sale and thought it looked pretty, totally unaware that it could cost him his head. I for one was certainly not going to report him to the First Sea Lord as he had been kind enough to let me tie up alongside but I did worry that others might not be so generous of spirit.

There had been an article in the Barge Association magazine, appropriately called Blue Flag - although that particular blue flag was something altogether different and used to indicate that you wanted to pass another vessel "wrong side", which outlined the rights and wrongs of flag etiquette. Ordinary mortals like me had to fly the British Merchant ship ensign, the red version or as it was known, the Red Duster. Amusingly, the front cover of that issue of the magazine showed a full colour photograph of a well-known DBA member on his Tjalk, under full sail, boldly flying on the stern a large Union Flag - totally taboo!

Whether that particular owner still has a head I can't say, but he was taking a terrible risk!

At Marseilles les Aubigny the following night I once again found nothing particularly illuminating, although it seemed to be a favourite nesting ground for some of the barging in-crowd. I had been suffering with a mild and irritating bout of (for want of a better term) groin rash, and we found a good pharmacy alongside the quay that after I had identified the problem to the nice young lady with a series of hand signs, sold me some cream.

Our medicine chest on board contained a variety of creams and potions for all sorts of ailments and diseases, but the problem was that most of them had been acquired in foreign parts - France, Belgium, Holland, Spain, Poland and Thailand for example.

Inconsiderate as it may seem, the descriptions of the contents of these tubes, bottles, sachets and pill dispensers, were all written in incomprehensible foreign languages. This was OK at first because the medication was immediately applied for the intended use. The problems arose when some remedy was required months after purchase and you had absolutely no idea which one was to be used for which particular deadly disease.

That is where Mike's not inconsiderable experience of matters medical came to the fore. He suggested that we need to stick a little label on each item at the time of purchase, and write on it clearly, in English, what it was for. Brilliant!

And that was how that day's acquisition came to be clearly labelled - "Betty Swollocks" and would never again be applied to a wasp sting or an athlete's foot. Quite amazing what can be achieved with a little expert advice.

We arrived at Cours les Barres at four in the afternoon to find all the moorings already occupied and TV aerials tuned in, presumably so that the wives could keep up to date with Neighbours or Properties Abroad or some other rubbish, but we managed to squeeze into a space about 2 inches longer than the boat. There was a floating oxymoron - a wide beam narrowboat in front of us called "Mr Blue Sky". All well and good but the result was that you had the bloody tune buzzing through your head for the next couple of hours. There are quite a number of boat owners who have chosen song titles for their boats, but it did usually mean that you spent the next few hours trying to get the tune out of your head. One such name graced a Dutch cruiser that I had noticed. It was called 'Steel Away' and although it probably had nothing to do with the song, I thought of the beautiful ballad of Finbar Furey called 'Steal Away'.

Another that particularly struck a chord (if you'll pardon the pun) with me was" The Rose of Tralee".

She was lovely and fair
Like the roses of the summer
It was not her beauty alone that won me
Oh no t'was the truth in her eyes ever shining
That made me love Mary
The Rose of Tralee

Strangely though, the owner had never heard of the song.

In England there was a hire-cum-timeshare company called Canal Time that operated a large fleet of boats, all of which had a number followed by a weird name that seemed to mean very little. I think that whoever dreamed up the names must have been on some dangerous hallucinatory drug - like Newcastle Brown Ale or something. You might come across a "Chapmans

29

Rusty" - No 204, or a "Jobi Red", "Scotts Wonder Wultz" or a "Holker End." There was even a number 69 - "Debbies Delight!"

Some of these boats cost over £1000 per week to hire. Who in their right mind would pay that sort of money to float around in public on a boat called "69 - Debbies Delight?" You would either have to be totally stupid, blissfully ignorant or possess a quirky sense of humour.

The other strange thing about these boats is that they had a solid steel front bulkhead, devoid of door or window. A friend of ours told me that as a past-time she had compiled a little book and written down the numbers 1 to 250. Each time they passed one of the Canal Time boats she would write the name alongside the number, hoping eventually to complete the set. Now Pauline was a rather prim and proper lady who had retired from a life-time behind the counter of a branch of Barclays Bank. It therefore came as a bit of a shock when she said to me one day, referring to these boats.

"We call them Anal Time."

"Why's that?" I asked innocently.

"Well, because you can only get in from the rear."

We turned left at Decize and descended the river lock. No sign of the belligerent lock-keeper that I'd nearly throttled the last time we were here. Somewhat surprisingly, we managed to find a mooring on the bottom of the Nivernais, and as you do when in France, dined in a Vietnamese restaurant.

From here it took us six days to get to Vincelles. Most of the trip passed without much to report. The canal dives in an out of the river Yonne after Merry sur Yonne and nearing Cravant we took a slight unplanned deviation when leaving the lock. There was a sharp left hand bend from the lock cut into the river and I think I got the stern a bit too close to the bank. This resulted in a complete loss of steerage leaving us stranded across the flow as the boat was slowly but surely turned completely about in the current, to be left facing downstream towards the weir! The channel here was too narrow to turn so I had to reverse 100 yards or so before I had enough room to get the boat facing in the right direction again. Nothing too desperate, but another example of how a slight distraction or lack of concentration can have worrying consequences.

At Chevroches we had an unexpected rendezvous with Richard the electrician and Lin, who had forsaken the life afloat for the grand tour by motorhome. There was another replica barge moored, "Charlotte" and we had a pleasant evening around the barbecue with Mike and Brenda, and Peter and Jean. Unable to pass up the opportunity, I prevailed on Richard's goodwill to have a look at the alternator, which I felt had not been charging as it should. Richard took it apart and cleaned the brushes which he said had started to stick and all was well thereafter. He showed me how to do it in case the need arose in the future and I watched carefully, took it all on board, and then a few days later, forgot everything I ever knew on the subject. I had always held the belief that the only thing you ever needed to know about electrics was where to find the on - off switch.

Later that day we were approaching another blind bend when a large grey floating missile came charging towards us, sweeping a mini tidal wave before it and sending surging wash rushing along the bank in its wake. It looked to me like a converted naval vessel - a Fast Patrol Boat or similar and seemed to be holding speed trials! I slowed down and moved to the right. We passed with about a metre or so between us and I gave the skipper the usual friendly acknowledgement. This was returned with a shake of the fist and a lot of arm waving.

"What was all that about?" Mike asked, and I honestly had no idea.

"Maybe Germans warning us about the next invasion," I suggested.

I turned around to give him some good old-fashioned British abuse but he had disappeared into the distance in a cloud of spray, leaving us bouncing around in his wash. Once more I found myself wishing that we were equipped with a couple of 4 inch guns.

When I first started boating on the English canals in the seventies, the Royal Navy operated a small fleet of narrowboats, disguised as warships. Quite what their purpose was I was never sure but the defence budget back then was obviously a bit more generous than it is now. The result of this was that you could be happily boating along the Grand Union without a care in the world, and come around a bend to find a six foot wide pocket battleship or a nuclear submarine heading towards you flat out in the middle of the cut steered by a drunken sailor out on a week's jolly. One thing was certain. You needed to keep well out of their way - these boys had absolutely no idea how to handle a boat.

We had another rather silly and unnecessary contretemps with a hire cruiser just before the final lock before Vincelles. I don't make a habit of holding up boats that are obviously faster than Saul Trader, but this guy had been irritating me for twenty minutes or so, coming up close to our stern and trying to squeeze past in places which were much too narrow. I knew that we were getting close to the lock and as I slowed for the approach, which was out of sight around a bend, he decided to make his move. Suddenly there he was, alongside and flat out. His wash caused Saul Trader to lose all steerage and we were swept out of control into the bank. As I shouted and swore at him, he suddenly realised that Oh dear there was a lock, firmly shut, right in front of him. With that he slammed his boat into reverse and skidded right across our bow before his stern hit the opposite bank and he bounced off, now facing in the opposite direction.

At that moment the gates opened and I slowly and cockily motored into the lock, giving him the flat palm message that he had been an impulsive idiot and it had got him nowhere. As we were mooring at the rally site alongside Pisgah he came roaring past in an apparent act of defiance sending waves crashing into all the moored boats and getting him several volleys of "friendly advice" from the assembled skippers.

As for the rally - well it was a rally! Generous helpings of bonhomie, cliques enjoying private drinks parties, barbecues on sterns, snobbish sideways glances from the owners of "traditional" barges towards the upstarts who had dared to attend with their cheap and nasty replicas and had the audacity to call themselves barge owners. You may laugh but I have heard of occasions when these boats were ostracised and told in no uncertain terms to moor away from the "proper" vessels. Saul Trader itself was of course a replica, having been built in England in 1990, but fortunately it was such a good replica that most people couldn't tell the difference and I had even been asked where in Holland it was built, even by Dutchmen, who had been amazed when I told them of its origins in the wilds of Gloucestershire.

Pat and Dobbo joined us for the fun. They had driven down in Dobbo's metallic green Mercedes SL 250. He had got it cheap, possibly because most people regarded green cars as unlucky - not the sort of ridiculous superstition that would put off Dobbo. Fifty years in insurance had taught him that the worst risks were teachers (one had telephoned him to ask whether changing tyres from cross-ply to radial would affect his no-claim bonus), social workers, teenage girls and civil servants. They were the enemy of the law-abiding motorist, regardless of the colour of their automobile. Most of the cars Dobbo had owned had brought with them more than his fair share of bad luck anyway.

Dobbo had even invested in a Tom Tom satellite navigation accessory, which he stuck proudly on the windscreen with a rubber sucker. Fortunately this meant that I could leave them to their own devices as to the route and the destination. Dobbo's hearing had got progressively worse. He had always been a bit suspect ,especially when it was suggested that it was his round - "he was so close with his money the he'd skin a fart and sell it to a Nun if he thought he could get away with it", but now it had extended to not hearing the nice young lady who told him, "at the next roundabout, take the second exit."

Pat had therefore had to shout the instructions as best he could, usually at the point where Dobbo had passed the second exit and was blindly heading for the third. Nevertheless the result was that exactly 3.30pm on the opening afternoon of the Vincelles rally a little luminous green Mercedes 250SL rolled into the car park and Pat and an elderly gentleman attempted valiantly to extricate themselves from the tiny cramped interior. Dobbo really should have known better at his age - these cars were designed for slim-line young studs who could flick themselves athletically from their mounts like agile jockeys, not for 80 year old six foot tall geriatrics with the agility of an elephant who took half an hour getting themselves out of bed in the mornings.

And so it was that after some twenty minutes of groaning, creaking, pulling and pushing, Dobbo was unceremoniously raised upright, somewhat shattering the illusion, to announce,

"Good trip, good trip - yep - never went wrong once."

Pat rolled his eyes and looked towards the heavens.

Satnav – by Pam Ayres (allegedly)

"I have a little Satnav, it sits there in my car.
A Satnav is a driver's friend it tells you where you are.
I have a little Satnav, i've had it all my life.
It's better than the normal ones, my Satnav is my wife.
It gives me full instructions, especially how to drive
"It's sixty miles an hour", it says, "You're doing sixty five".
It tells me when to stop and start, and when to use the brake
And tells me that it's never ever, safe to overtake.
It tells me when a light is red, and when it goes to green
It seems to know instinctively, just when to intervene.
It lists the vehicles just in front, and all those to the rear.
And taking this into account, it specifies my gear.
I'm sure no other driver, has so helpful a device.
For when we leave and lock the car, it still gives its advice.
It fills me up with counselling, each journey's pretty fraught.
So why don't I exchange it, and get a quieter sort?
Ah well, you see, it cleans the house, makes sure I'm properly fed.
It washes all my shirts and things, and keeps me warm in bed!
Despite all these advantages, and my tendency to scoff,
I only wish that now and then, I could turn the bugger off."

Rob's friend Michael with his lovely retriever Daisy, and one of Joe's sons, Sam, with his gorgeous girlfriend Jo, joined us for a barbecue and we formed a friendly little clique of our own. The sun shone and all in all we had a pleasant weekend, in spite of Rob's misgivings concerning rally "jollies". Pat developed a rather unhealthy crush on Robert - or to be more precise on Robert's boat. He virtually abandoned our company and went to live on Pisgah. It was the machinery in particular, rather than Robert that held this fatal attraction. Pisgah, as well as having its original and apparently rare marine-build Gardner 5LW as the main means of propulsion, was also equipped with a vintage water-cooled Petter generator, which when started would fill the air for miles around with black acrid smoke and shatter the peace of anyone who happened to be less than half a mile away. That is, of course, when it started. Rob had developed muscles like Charles Atlas from endlessly winding away at the starting handle to little or no avail - and that is where Pat came in. He had spent most of his life with fishing boats on the beach at Hastings and was a bit of a self-taught genius with engines.

He soon had the genny spitting fire and causing the deaf to hear, the vibration sending Pisgah rocking from side to side. Even Dobbo had to shield his ears! Pat then turned his attentions to Rob's 1950's Seagull outboard that hadn't turned its prop for over ten years and within half an hour had it spluttering away in that inimitable way of Seagull outboards. The acid test was to see whether it could do its stuff on the back of a rubber boat, so we blew up our Avon Rover and spent the rest of the day zooming around the rally site in ever-decreasing circles, upsetting the peace and quiet of the assembled masses.

Dobbo was so enthralled that he fell asleep in a chair. Even at the ripe old age of 80, Dobbo still had jet black hair (we reckoned he was sponsored by Cherry Blossom Black) and the heat of the afternoon sun had started to melt the illusion, leaving little steaks of black oozing down behind his ears. The large bald spot in the middle, something that Dobbo had never actually seen, gaily reflecting the light.

In the afternoon a strange Paganesque ritual took place in the form of a contest between the local French and the British invaders - a sort of latter day Anglo-French war that I sincerely hoped wouldn't last for a hundred years! This involved grown men parading around with their balls in small bags which they took out and shamelessly displayed in front of women and innocent children. They have a piste in the open and start rubbing their balls before tossing them in the air at a much smaller puny little ball - this all accompanied by much cheering and encouragement from the women. Some of the more aggressive amongst them actually aimed their balls at others and seemingly tried to smash them into the dust. After they had all tossed off, they stood around admiring their work and sometimes even measured the size of them.

This disgusting habit has spread around the world and has apparently been going on unchecked since early Egyptian times. I have recently seen it in Spain, presumably imported by bored British retirees with bugger all else to do with their time. When the tannoy announced that more British participants were needed, Dobbo sprang from his dozing like a child at Christmas. As a leading member of the Black Dog Petanque team, runners up in the East Sussex League Division 3 1992 season, Dobbo saw his chance for glory. I'm not sure whether this practice involved rules, but even if there were any, Dobbo would have dismissed them as an unnecessary encumbrance. Dobbo knew all the ways to cheat and manipulate and would be instrumental in a single-handed defeat of the damned Frenchies for once and for all. He strode purposefully over to the arena and barged his way on to the pitch,

"Membership number," demanded a stout woman in stout shoes.

"What's that?" Dobbo enquired.

I think he probably knew what a membership number was and his question was a sort of rhetorical plea for a repeat of the question. What she was trying to tell him was that this competition was open solely for those who were active and fully paid-up members of the Kennet & Avon Canal Society of which Dobbo was not. He did point out that he had something of a reputation in the game and could probably have the thing sewn up with a historic victory, but his protestations were in vain. He even suggested turning traitor and playing for the French but was told that he needed to be an active and fully paid-up member of Les Amis du Canal du Nivernais, of which Dobbo was also not. He did have the final say though and told them that they could stick their balls up their arse.

The following day Rob had a miraculous change of heart on rallies - the pointlessness in general and of the types that attended them in particular, when a sexy young lady from the local TV station asked him to give a live interview. Rob spoke pretty passable French for a Sheffielder, and threw himself into the task with gusto. Lights and cameras were set up and the show was ready to roll. Rob's socks and underpants flapping about on the washing line behind them seemed to provide a fitting backdrop. Then Pat, unaware of the impending action, decided to make sure the generator would still start. Consternation, black smoke and excruciating noise accompanied desperate shouts of Cut Cut - somebody stop that bloody engine - take two (in French). Pat pulled on the engine stop - and it came off in his hand. Another frantic few minutes passed in confusion before they managed to locate the cut off and stop the racket and peace was restored.

The interview was of course in French, but judging by the smiles and gestures of goodwill. I imagined that Rob was telling them how wonderful it all was, how marvellous to see such a crowd and what a pleasure it was to attend such a friendly gathering and meet such a lot of like-minded and interesting people. Bloody hypocrite!

In the evening we enjoyed a communal dinner in the marquee and Joe Parfitt gave a speech welcoming the Kennet & Avon contingent. More speeches thanking Joe for his tireless work for the Nivernais Friends and for organising the wonderful rally.

This was followed by various presentations of goodwill and the awarding of a magnificent trophy to the winners of the Petanque competition - the French.

"Balls," was Dobbo's only comment.

38

Lights , Camera....Action! Rob in his element

The weekend was rounded off with a spectacular firework display which illuminated a dark and threatening sky - but luckily the rain held off. The consensus seemed to be that the weekend had been a resounding success.

After the rally we returned south for a few days accompanied by Rob on Pisgah, with Pat as Chief Engineer, partly to give Pat and Dobbo a taste of the Nivernais, but also to pay a visit to another of Joe's sons, Herbie, who ran a boat repair business at Mailly la Ville. I had been having a bit of trouble with one of the toilet pumps and Herbie had acquired a replacement Jabsco unit for only about double the price in the UK. I paid up gratefully and then discovered the following day that the problem was not the pump at all but a simple fuse. So c'est la vie. I now have a spare Jabsco pump ready for the next breakdown. (*that was eight years ago and I still have it - patiently waiting for the next breakdown!*).

Needless to say, we didn't see a lot of Pat over the next few days, as he ensconced himself in Pisgah's engine room with his new-found love, the Gardiner 5LW. Rob let him steer the boat from time to time and he unfortunately discovered one of Pisgah's little quirks when he attempted taking the boat into a

39

lock. The gear lever was arse about face. In less nautical terms this meant that when you put the lever forward, the boat went backwards. All very well if you remember that, but in the heat of the moment and approaching a fragile looking plastic hire boat in a lock it is quite easy to forget - particularly when, as in this case, you pull the lever back hoping to stop! By chance there was a heavy gate immediately ahead which rattled and shook as Pisgah was brought to an inelegant halt.

We made a lunch stop under the cliffs at Le Saussois and Pat and I climbed to the top in blistering heat to admire the fantastic view of the river valley and the village of Merry sur Yonne. There was a path of sorts with a few steps hacked into the rock and it was very steep in places, but, I hasten to add, we were not on any of the "proper" climbers routes, classified by the UK Climbers website with mysterious codes like F8c and 7A+. There were a few hardy grimpeurs spread-eagled against the scorched rock face like chit chat lizards, their lives held by a thread - well by a length of rope attached to a rusty bolt to be more specific.

Dobbo declined the experience.

"I've climbed hundreds of cliffs," he explained, "hundreds and hundreds. They're all the same."

Now Dobbo was getting on for 80 and all he really needed to say was that at his age the cliff was too bloody steep and there was no way he was going up. But no, with true Dobbo never-admit-you're-beat philosophy, he had to explain it away as being too old hat and boring to bother about! I took a photo of him from the top - a miniature Dobbo reposing on the deck, soulless and staring into the void - probably thinking about all those boring cliffs he'd climbed in the past.

After a couple of days of leisurely cruising we arrived at Clamecy and breasted up with Pisgah inside the small basin, where we stayed for three nights before heading back to Migennes. Dobbo took the train to Vincelles to retrieve his car - amazingly he achieved this all on his own even though it entailed a change of train in Cravant. We had a very pleasant farewell dinner and the following morning Pat said a tearful farewell - to the Gardner - and off they went. "At the end of the road turn right." No Dobbo, that's LEFT."

I had ordered 1000 litres of diesel from a firm in Vaux but although we waited for over two hours after the appointed time, the tanker never arrived. At Auxerre we had a surprise visit from none other than the designer and builder of Saul Trader himself - Phil Trotter. Phil had been to a motorcycle rally in Italy on his ancient Laverda and stayed for a couple of nights. He was a keen latter-day rocker and served as the Entertainment Office for the UK Laverda Owners Group. The Bald, Beard and Beer Gut Brigade. He once said that he had been recommended to sound out a pub in Devon for one of their weekend gatherings. It was The Black Cock in South Moulton.

"I didn't get very far," Phil told me, "You ever tried putting "black cock" into Google?"

We met up again with Alain and his Thai wife Porn, and invited them to the boat for a barbecue. We were tied opposite the Cathedral in what must be one of the most impressive mooring sites in the whole of France. In the morning Phil bade us farewell and puttered off on his long journey back to Gloucester (I suggested he wrote a follow-up to the legendary tome written by an army officer of his days in the Horse Guards. "Fifty Years in the Saddle" by Major R Soar), and then we too cast off for the short trip to Migennes.

As we arrived, Joe came down to the river and indicated where he wanted us to tie up. I turned the boat against the current in one sweep, the bow gently nudging in to the bank, before easing a bit of throttle to bring it obediently alongside. Joe grabbed the bow line and actually complimented me on the manoeuvre - rare praise indeed from the great man.

Here we left the boat for two months before returning at the end of September for a mini epic voyage to Holland.

The Cliffs at Saussois with Saul Trader far below

Tucked in tight at Clamecy

Chapter 3   Migennes - Dordrecht

Saul Trader was due for a dry-docking and a hull blacking. It had last been out of the water at St Jean four years ago. There was a dry dock at Migennes which was operated by Joe but unfortunately our draft, which I had always thought was 1 metre, although this had never been checked, was assumed to be too deep for the entrance cill. Quite why I decided to take the boat all the way to Holland for the work I'm not really sure. Michael Mortimer, who we had met at Vincelles, had regularly used a guy who shall remain nameless, Otto, who had a yard in Alpen an der Rhin, a short distance from Dordrecht. I spoke on the 'phone to this anonymous person who thought he would be able to crane out Saul Trader and so we arranged to meet in Gorinchem (pronounced Gokkphlegm, or something like that) to discuss what needed to be done.

And anyway, it did seem a good idea at the time and a bit of an adventure: so on the 23rd September 2009, we, that is myself, Mike (he of the blowing of the tubes) and Ner-Ner- Ner-Nicholas Hill (he of the famous stutter and the nb Jaguar and 60's carrying for Willow Wren and Ashby Canal Transport), set out from Migennes and headed northward on the River Yonne. I would have preferred to go via the River Sambre, to Namur and the Meuse route to Holland, but unfortunately due to the collapse of a little insignificant aqueduct halfway along the route at Vadencourt, the Sambre was closed as a through route, and would in fact remain so for many years. When first closed in 2006 it was reported that it would stay closed for 2 years. In 2018 it is still closed. Nick was a bit of a boat addict - well a boat steering addict to be exact. I think it stemmed from his days as a young lad when he would stand on the towpath near Rugby to watch the working boats go by. He got to know some of the captains and would always try to blag a ride. After a while the captains would give him charge of the tiller while they made the tea or stoked the range and eventually he got more and more confident and would be left to steer for miles, even being allowed to take the boats through locks and tunnels. I remember seeing some footage of working boats where a young boy who was steering a loaded boat, danced a jig on the back deck and even did somersaults over the tiller bar. I don't know whether that was Nick but if it had been I wouldn't have been at all surprised.

Whenever he found himself on a boat, whatever the size, he wouldn't be able to stop himself asking for a "go" on the wheel. Now that he'd retired, his idea of a good day out was to drive from the Midlands to Yorkshire, then cycle along the Aire & Calder Canal just to try to catch a commercial barge for a ride and hopefully, a steer. He had steered a puffer in Scotland, a short boat in Leeds, a paddle steamer on Lake Lucerne, a long-tail boat on the Chao Phraya river in Bangkok and for all I know, the Queen Mary 2. I think he kept a little book and marked off all the boats and barges he'd steered, rather like we used to do when we had "cabbed" a steam locomotive. He told me that he had spent a week on the Rhine with the owner of one of the large hotel cruise ships that ply between Amsterdam and Budapest. He had been left in charge for a couple of days when the owner had some other business to attend to, and Nick was appointed temporary "Captain." I should add here that the ship was empty at the time and not carrying passengers. Nick told me that he had needed to rebuke some young upstart in the crew when he tried to tell him which side of a buoy to pass.

"I t, t,t told him to mind his own b,b,business. I was the Captain - the owner had quite c,c,c,categorically told me that I was in charge."

At St Mammés I managed to get 1000 litres of diesel from the Ateliers and we ate well in the local café with our old mate Gil, who had been running a 350 ton peniche single-handed for thirty years, and had a few tales to tell - cor bloody 'ell agh. After an eleven hour run the following day, covering 87 kilometres and 7 locks on the Seine, we moored for the night for 44 Euros in the Bassin d'Arsenal. As it turned out I could have saved the 44 Euros had I had the foresight to have my VHF switched on and tuned in to Channel 10. Moored across

44

the river were "Pedro" and "Floan", two 38 metre commercial peniches owned and operated by English couples. Pedro I had encountered many years earlier and was mentioned in despatches in my second book of our misadventures. Floan was run by George and Helen Smith. I had met Helen many years earlier when she was the steerer on a GLC sponsored narrowboat giving holidays to wayward kids. She was a tough and spirited lady who called a spade a spade and could give as good as she got in any company. They had also worked for UCC on the English waterways with a motor and butty. We met Helen in the evening in the Place de la Bastille and the first thing she did was have a go at me for not having my VHF switched on.

"I've been calling you all day on Channel 10 - why don't you listen to your radio. All boaters must listen on Channel 10. What do you think it's for - show!! We were trying to tell you that could moor alongside us for the night."

I think that since that day the first thing I have ever done on starting up is to switch on my radio and tune into Channel 10.

The four of us - me, Mike, Nick, and Helen, sat outside a busy bar beneath the Colonne de Juillet with its wonderful golden statue, the Spirit of Freedom, commemorating the 1830 Revolution, looking down on us. Helen and Nick caught up with happenings canal on both sides of the Channel, berating the idiots of BW and the idiots of the VNF with equal intensity and with a volume that increased as the evening progressed. When l'addition was presented, Nick almost choked on the last few dregs of his beer, .

"Fer-fer-fer-fucking hell," he spluttered, Eighty fer fer fer four fer fer fer - fucking Euros!"

We had had two small beers each. Helen didn't help matters when she said.

"Well - if you'd've had your VHF on you could've moored over with us and there's a bar round the corner where the beer's two Euros a pint."

"We could've got totally ber ber ber bolloxed for eighty four Euros," said Nick.

"Yeah but I bet it isn't Carlsberg, " muttered Mike.

"I bet if Carlsberg made VHF radios, they'd be the best VHF radios in the World", I suggested, "they would probably bloody well switch themselves on automatically."

Nick had once spent a couple of weeks with Helen and George on the Floan and was most put out that George wouldn't let him anywhere near the wheel.

We were putting in some lengthy shifts - 10 and 11 hours a day - greatly helped by the fact that both Nick and Mike were able to help out with the steering.

A couple of miles before the turning at Fargniers, which would take us on to the Ste Quentin Canal we were held up for fifteen minutes or so by a loaded peniche. I was steering and Nick kept telling me to overtake. In my opinion there was neither enough room or sufficient visibility but still Nick persisted.

"Go on you can ge ge ge get by him," he insisted.

I ignored him for as long as I could before I said.

"Nick. When you were the "Captain" on the Rhine you wouldn't let anyone tell you what to do so please don't try telling me."

That shut him up and a few minutes later the peniche slowed and moved over to the right and the skipper waved us through.

We worked two hour "watches" and in just three days we arrived at the Requeval Tunnel entrance on the Canal Ste Quentin, just 20 minutes after the last passage of the day. Although we were making excellent progress, we were of course restricted by the operating hours of the écluses, which at that time of the year, were closing at 7.00pm. In the heyday of canal carrying in England, the working boatman would think nothing of doing 16 or 17 hour days, with a motor and butty, loaded with fifty tons, about an inch of freeboard, and a crew of two. Nicholas still lived in those times - I suppose he was what is now known as retro. He sported a 50's bri-nylon shirt with the sleeves rolled up to the elbows and a scowling expression topped off with a flat cap. He wore shorts well into November with a dashing pair of sandals and grey socks. Nick was a dedicated follower of fashion - 1950's fashion.

When he looked after the large Woolwich motor "Birmingham" for me in the 1990's, he would thrash it around as though his life, and his wages (though he wasn't actually getting any), depended on it. This practice did upset some of the nouveau boating fraternity at times in their glossy painted gin palaces.

"Fer fer Floating bloody ca-ca-caravans," he called them or "floating bloody cof-cof-coffins" for those who chose to bedeck their rooftops with plants and flowers. I once asked him whether he ever "watched his wash", something that the modern day boater was constantly reminded to do and he thought for a moment before saying.

"Yeah - sometimes when I got a bit bored I would watch it fer - fer - fer flooding over the ter - ter - ter towpath."

"C-c-c-cuts finished," he would moan, "might as well con-con - concrete the lot of it and turn it into a mer- mer -motorway!"

Overnight a loaded peniche had arrived and tied up astern of us, so gently that we didn't know it was there until the morning. The "Surf-Bord", as it was called, was directed to connect his lines to the tunnel tug and we were pulled along behind. At the other end, he soon moved over and indicated for us to overtake him, or, as Nick's would say, in the language of the working boatman, to "loose us by". By three o'clock that afternoon we were moored in the Hero's harbour at Cambrai behind another old acquaintance from boating in England, Bill Fisher. Bill was a long-time champion of the English waterways and as a founder member of the Kennet & Avon Canal Society, had been instrumental in getting the restoration of the entire length from Bristol to Reading off the ground. He had accompanied the Queen herself on the "Rose of Hungerford" at Caen Hill locks for the grand opening in 1990. He now had an established canalside business in Newbury which included moorings and chandlery as well as a dry dock and full boat building and repair facilities. I had spoken to Bill when bringing Saul Trader through the tricky King's Lock at Newbury in flood conditions some years earlier when he had advised me to go through backwards - very wisely as it turned out.

He was now in France cruising on his 1927 Luxemotor, "Rijnstroom", which he had purchased as a hull in Holland and towed to Newbury where he had converted it with accommodation and fitted an engine. Bill kindly offered to give us a lift to the station so that we could go back to Migennes

47

and pick up my car and I silently hoped his barge steering was better than his driving as we almost went the wrong way round a roundabout and narrowly avoided a collision with a taxi. The train journey took five and three quarter hours (three and a half to drive) and involved a taxi dash across Paris from the Nord station to Paris Bercy. The train into Paris Nord was 20 minutes late which left us about half an hour for the 7 kilometre taxi ride - and Paris in the middle of the day, or at any other time come to that, is not the easiest city to travel through at speed. We inched our way around the Place de la Bastille and Nick was heard to mutter.

"Thank G G G God we haven't got time to stop for a beer."

We made the connection with two minutes to spare.

Three weeks later, we all returned, - me, Nick and Mike once again, to complete the second leg of our voyage to Holland. I picked them up at a small village near Ashford in Kent, where Mike was to leave his car with a friend. We lodged overnight at the Premier Inn on the A20 and were on the 0700 Norfolk Line ferry "Dover Seaways" to Dunkirk, where we indulged ourselves with a full English.

One of the obvious advantages of boating in the Northern half of France is the shorter journeys from the Channel ports. By midday we were back on board Saul Trader and starting to make ready to sail on the following morning tide. We headed north on the Canal de Saint Quentin to the Bassin Rond, avoiding the connection at Estrun with the Canal du Nord to keep straight on through Valenciennes to Montagne du Nord. The busy, straight and wide commercial waterway, the Canal du Nord, was started before the First World War but the work was abandoned after much severe bomb damage and not completed until the 1960's. It was built to carry larger vessels with a capacity of 650 tons and connect the Seine with the northern regions of France. I have never sampled its delights, but I think it is probably a fairly boring 93 kilometres. Another prominent member of the DBA, Bob Marsland, said that he hated it with a passion. However it's now already past its sell-by date and there are plans well underway to construct a brand new waterway with a capacity to carry ships of over 4000 tons, to connect the Dunkirk-Escaut Canal with the Oise river at

Compiegne. Work is scheduled to start in 2017 and expected to take six years. It is a massive and futuristic project and will be equipped with five or more inter-modal hubs connecting the canal to the existing rail freight network.

Well, so what! We can just about carry 20 tons on our good old English canals - when there's enough water in the cut, that is!

The short cut through the Scarpe Inferieur, which I had tried unsuccessfully to navigate some years earlier, was still closed so we had to use the Haut Escaut route into Belgium, turning right at the Canal Nimy-Blaton-Peronnes, a deep and straight waterway that took us through just two large locks to Mons, where we moored once again in the Grand Large for fifteen Euros. At Seneffe we turned left on to the Bruxelles Canal and the Ronquierres boat lift. There was still only one caisson working (surprise surprise) but we didn't arrive until after closing time and tied up at the top. In the morning we had been joined by several other boats but luckily managed to get in on the first downhill working behind two peniches. We made good progress through the narrow channel at Halle past the railway station where the TGV's still raced through, and the Brussels outskirts but our fortune came to a bit of a hiatus at the lock at Zemst. There was a red light and we tied up to wait for an ascending commercial to enter the lock with painful precision and eventually creep forward. We let go the ropes and started away from the quay, but the light never changed and after a few minutes the gates closed ahead of us. I sounded the horn and waved somewhat fruitlessly at the lock-keeper but there was no way he was going to let us through before he re-set the lock for a second uphill commercial. I failed to see the logic in this as we were virtually seconds away from the lock and emptying would take exactly the same amount of time with us in it as it would do without us. However it became obvious that he wasn't going to budge so we tied up again and patiently waited for the second commercial to appear and be locked through. Then, when "Minerva" finally made her way sedately out of the lock it took another ten minutes before the lock-keeper remembered we were there and gave us a green. We had been held for nearly an hour and a half, completely unnecessarily in my opinion, and it was now past five o'clock and starting to get dark. When we had nestled alongside the wall and tossed a rope over a bollard I gave him the sort of scowl that would probably cause him to have a week off work for counselling.

We were trying to get to Willebroek, where there was a lock down into the tidal River Rupel. The last time we had been this way, coming from the other direction, the lock was closed for repair, but that had been several years ago and I was hoping that by now the work had been finished. The Brussels Canal through Willebroek is narrow and passes right through the centre of the town. As we approached, the weather closed in suddenly and dramatically and it started to sheet with rain. There are a number of low bridges where small local roads cross and it became almost impossible to pick them out. We switched on the Nav lights and slowed to a crawl, everybody straining to see the way ahead. Then through the gloom we spotted a red light. At first it was difficult to tell whether it was a traffic light or something more important. We were virtually stopped now. The visibility was so bad that the binoculars didn't help and the rain slashed across the windows. We drifted for a while, unable to work out exactly where we were. It was just possible to pick out the sides by the misted yellow street lights and while we were contemplating trying to moor the light ahead suddenly blinked green and a voice boomed out on the VHF, frightening us half to death.

"Come past the bridge - quickly please," ordered the mystery voice.

I inched the boat slowly forward in to the darkness while Mike and Nick stood outside on either side of the wheelhouse as lookouts. Suddenly a red light appeared high up to our left - I instinctively put the engine astern and then Mike shouted.

"It's his port light - I think it's a coaster or something pretty big. You're OK as you are but don't go anymore left."

Then the VHF interrupted the silence again.

"Keep your course and keep coming through the bridge."

As we did so a large black object filled the night and I could just make out the towering bow and then the bridge of the ship that was stopped just a few feet it seemed from our port side. It was probably a tanker on the way to the Port of Brussels but it was almost impossible to tell. We gradually moved past and Mike said.

"I presume that was the pilot on the radio - sounded English. But anyway I think we're clear now - bit close though."

We had got past the ship and somehow negotiated the bridge. It was a bit too close for comfort and I steered towards a group of lights which had appeared on our right. Suddenly I could see railings and then we nudged the wall.

"That's it," I said, "don't know whether we can moor here or not but we're going to anyway."

Nick jumped ashore with a bow rope and amazingly found a bollard and with a bit of left wheel the stern came obediently alongside. I saw another bollard and lassoed it with a short rope. We were there - although quite where there was I wasn't exactly sure.

When we had got our bearings back together, showered, shampooed and shaved, we decided to have a look at our immediate environment and found that we were in a very central part of Willebroek, with several restaurants and takeaway establishments within easy reach, which was just as well as the rain continued as a deluge. We decided on the old favourite Belgian fall-back of burger and frites with a liberal dollop of mayonnaise washed down with a couple of Amstel beers, and then discovered a nearby disco-cum-bar which looked a bit welcoming, with bright lights and warmth. After a few more beers and a bit of banter with some friendly locals, even Nick started to get into the groove. He pestered the disc jockey to play his favourite song - a song he knew simply as "the bicycle song."

I had heard this story once or twice in the past, It basically involved some frivolity in the Jolly Sailor at Berkhamstead in about 1967, probably on their way back from a jam'ole run, when Trevor (Maggoty) Maggs - Nick had a disparaging nickname for everyone, not sure what mine was, "Appy Arris" maybe - had spent half his wages playing this "bicycle song" on the juke box. Now exactly which bicycle song he was referring to was anybody's guess, and it certainly wasn't amongst the collection of discs of the DJ in the Crazy Diamond nightclub in Willebroek, who probably hadn't been a twinkle in his father's

51

eye in 1967. Thinking about it, even his mother probably hadn't been a twinkle in her father's eye either back in 1967. Nevertheless Nick insisted that the beleaguered DJ must have it somewhere in his collection of records.

My mate Ma Ma Maggoty Mike wants the bi bi bi bicycle song. You must no no know it. It goes .... Then he gave an inebriated rendition of something that was a cross between Beethoven's Ode to Joy and The Rolling Stones Brown Sugar and at that point we decided it was time to get him safely back to his bunk before he did any more damage to our relationship with the Crazy Diamond. We never did find out which song he was referring to - the nearest we could get to it was Melanie's 1967 hit "I've Got a Brand New Pair of Roller Skates that began with the line

"I rode my bicycle past your window last night."

Well it was about the right era I suppose.

The following morning dawned bright and clear. After a swift visit to the baker's we were off through the ornate vertical lift bridge, known as the Bridge of Peace which was built in 1952 after its forerunner was destroyed during World War 2. Shortly after this the main line bears to the left leading to the Schelde and a short arm now used as a small yacht basin leads to the lock, which would lower us on to the tidal River Rupel. Near the junction there is a small monument dedicated to the bateliers who had served and died for their Country during the two World Wars. Luckily the lock had been re-opened which saved us a detour of around 15 kilometres. The friendly lock-keeper assured us that any tidal flow on the Rupel was minimal and indeed, although we were going against it, we still managed a healthy 8 kilometres per hour and by 1.00pm we were safely moored on the pontoon at Lier (pronounced phlegm !).We did walk into the town to look up our friend Tine but the bar was closed.

After a few more miles the following morning we entered the last lock that would take us up into the busy Albert Canal. This is a veritable shipping motorway that connects Antwerp with the Meuse. The last time I had been on this stretch with Malcolm we had been beset with diesel problems and had a pretty traumatic few hours with the engine stopping several times leaving us helplessly bobbing around amongst the huge commercials. It had been a bit like being stranded in the middle lane of the M25 in rush-hour. I had spent the past couple of days regaling Mike and Nick with stories of the hundreds of ships we would be dicing with on the 10 kilometre section to Herentals and Nick was getting almost orgasmic with the thought. So it was, in true sod's law fashion, that we passed exactly three vessels in the entire trip. Nick's disappointment was palpable - he looked like the lad who had stood on the platform at Grantham for several hours waiting to video the Flying Scotsman passing through only to have his view totally blocked out by a dirty smelly Cross Country Voyager going in the opposite direction.

After the six locks at Herentals, we made good time as we entered Dutch waters and the Kanal van Bocholt, where the locks were very few and far between and the canals were deep and straight which did mean that we could put the hammer down through the flat and largely uninteresting terrain. Our progress was slowed only by the occasional manned swing bridge and after overnighting in Neerpelt and Veghel, where we arrived in darkness and had to tie up right next to a transport hub where lorries came and went all through the night, we swung left on to the Zuidwillemsvaart and the large lock at S'Hertogenbosch, gateway to the mighty Dutch river network that connects Rotterdam to the Rhine and Eastern Europe. We had to wait for over an hour while the lock-keeper packed in four large commercials for the descent. When the gates finally opened it seemed as though they were all being a bit over-polite. After you - no you go first - oh no please after you. It was like old ladies at a roundabout but they eventually sorted themselves out, edging their way past, and we got the green light.

At the first junction with the Maas we had to wait for two mighty container ships and a tanker to pass on their way south before making a dash across to the relative shelter of the right bank, bouncing and rolling in the wash. Another lock in the connecting cut between the Maas and the Waal, which we shared with two more 1500 tonners and we were hard to port and heading west on the Boven Merwede - over a dozen ships at a time in our sights, before we eventually spotted the entry channel which led to what looked like an impossibly small lock that took us up once more into the haven that is the small basin at Gorinchem, at a cost of 20 Euros per night - small price I suppose for the refuge from the hectic shipping channels and right in the centre of this very Dutch town.

Would you believe it! There sitting quietly alongside the wall was the R W Davis replica Northwich narrowboat "Morse", built at Saul by Mr Trotter and his merry men and taken by road to Holland where the new owner was living. I 'phoned Phil to tell him about our sighting, and it transpired that Craig (who used to be Scragg) had been over to do a few small jobs on it just a few days earlier. I was fond of Craig, who had started at the yard at about the same time as Wat Tyler and Saul Trader were started and he had accompanied us on many trips in the past. I was very sorry that we had missed him.

The next day Otto, who as I have said before shall remain nameless for legal reasons, came with his oppo Pieter to look at the boat. It was soon apparent that there was no way they were going to be able to lift Saul Trader out of the water at their yard at Alphen so that idea went straight out of the window and another yard at Dordrecht was suggested - Den Breejen. Otto said they were a well-respected company and would allow him to do the small jobs on the thrusters while the boat was in the dock - something that I would later come to regret.

I called the office of Den Breejen the following day and arranged to meet them. They did say that they wouldn't be able to start any work until the spring so I needed to find somewhere relatively close to leave Saul Trader for the winter. There were several small havens in Dordrecht so we decided to go and have a look for availability. Dordrecht is sited in a busy water junction, connecting the routes from the south on the Rhine with the ports of Rotterdam and the Hook. We dodged across the wide expanse of the Beneden Merwede channel from right to left between ocean going container ships, push tows with up to four massive barges in the consist and the ever present superfast ferries that buzzed around like water boatmen, and crept into the entrance of our old friend, the Wolververshaven. The lady bridge-keeper may have remembered us because she immediately raised the bridge and in we went, mixing nonchalantly with the ancient inhabitants as if we owned the place - no questions asked. The next exercise involved retrieving the car from Cambrai and this proved a bit of a challenge. The distance was about 165 miles by road but of course the trains didn't follow a direct route. My journey involved three changes - at Antwerp, Courtrai and Lille and took nearly five hours. Rather curiously, this was faster than the "fast" service which required reservations and was routed via Brussels and Lille. Although these services used TGV's and the Dutch Thalys high speed trains which were capable of 320 kph, for most of the way they ran at normal track speeds of little more than 120 kph. It amused me to watch the read out display that showed the speed. What was the point of telling passengers they were travelling at 75 miles an hour - freight trains went faster than that. Better to keep your mouth shut and let them think they're going sub-sonic!

I drove back to Dordrecht in two hours, and found Nick and Mike exactly where I expected them - propped up against a very cosy and lively dockside bar. The old town around the various havens in Dordrecht is wonderfully preserved and atmospheric. Unauthorised vehicles are kept off the streets by automatic barrier posts that raise and lower when you have the requisite pass key. Sometimes they stayed down in the ground and it was difficult to know if you could pass or not. If you chanced it and the thing started to rise up as you went over it you could end up with some rather expensive damage to your undercarriage. Even with these restrictions there were far too many vehicles and hardly any free parking space - and you needed to watch out for the hundreds of bicycles that clattered and jingled around - many of them the old traditional Dutch sit-up-and-beggers, with their wicker shopping baskets and their long-limbed lady riders with arrow straight backs. Some of them had little two-wheeled trailers humming along behind, and many with a small child in an oversize pink crash hat sitting in the pillion seat, gazing nonchalantly about.

There were lots of interesting individual shops - antiques, model trains and general bric a brac all adding to the intrigue, and of course the coffee shops with their pungent sweet smelling aromas that reminded me of Isle of Wight festivals. I drove over to Den Breejen's yard the next day and agreed to a complete blasting back to steel for the whole of the boat, top, bottom and decks, and a total repaint. Cost? - don't even ask. I'll just say that if I sell a couple of million copies of this book it might just about cover it!

It was obvious that we wouldn't be allowed to stay in the Wolververshaven for the winter but there was another basin adjacent called the Nieuwe Haven, which wasn't so fussy about the age or heritage of your vessel, as long as you had the money to pay. We negotiated with the friendly young havenmeester, who showed us to a good pontoon mooring close to the entrance where we left Saul Trader for the five months until the end of March. We had arranged a slot with Den Breejen for the following April.

Chapter 4

Traumas & Joys of Shipyards

So it was that in the spring of 2010, towards the end of March I met up with Mike in Harwich and after a Brewers Fayre pie and chips and a couple of pints, we boarded the 23.00 Stena Line sailing to the Hook of Holland, where we arrived after a reasonable night's kip, thanks to the comfort of a double cabin, suitably refreshed at 08.00 hours. Although the traffic was pretty heavy at that time of the day, we arrived at the Nieuwe Harbour at Dordrecht by about 10.30. We spent the rest of the day de-winterising the boat and cleaning up after the long Dutch winter, before retiring to the bar, and just before we left for Den Breejen the next morning, I managed to block up the bloody heads. There was no time to look at them as we had arranged to be at the yard at 1.00pm and so we gingerly nosed our way out of the Nieuwe Haven into the Oude Rhin, passing below the massive stern of a commercial that had moored on the bunker pontoon outside the entrance. I waited while he settled alongside as I'd had experience of being thrown around in the wash of these giants thrashing their props around as they eased their sterns into a mooring, rather like a broody hen sitting on her eggs. We then turned right to head up the Beneden Merwede towards the yard, which I thought was about five kilometres upstream. At least we didn't have to cross the channel as the basin we needed was on the right hand side, but we still had to watch out for the waterbuses, skidding and sliding into their respective bus stops, and keep an eye over our shoulder for any large commercials racing up behind.

I had a rough idea where the yard was situated. We did have an address but that's not a lot of use when you're on the water side of a premises. There were several small basins and inlets on both sides of the river, many of them used for commercial shipping repair work and it was difficult to know which one was Mr Breejen. After about five kilometres we saw what I thought might be the basin that we were looking for. There were no signs or indications but we turned in anyway, as much

57

in hope as expectation. There was a 1000 tonner moored on the right against a line of dolphins. As we motored slowly past the "Elionie", a figure emerged from the massive shed ahead of us and started to beckon us on. We had arrived, and by chance this seemed to be the right place - more by luck than judgement I have to say.

This "shed" was a cavernous covered space and we were excitedly waved forward into the darkness almost to the far end, when several men shouted for us to take their lines and pulled us this way and that until we were positioned exactly where they wanted us. I looked behind and into the very same shed behind us motored Elionie, all 70 metres and 1000 tons of her. The same routine - lines thrown and secured, ship centrally positioned - all done with a quiet efficiency. I asked Mike to hold the fort while I dived below to look at the toilet which I had blocked, and I hadn't been down there for more than five minutes when he called down.

"Don't empty the bog will you - we're dried out".

I couldn't believe it. I ran up to the wheelhouse and there we were, sitting on dry concrete. The entire shed was in fact a floating dock, 100 metres long by 14 metres wide, and was lifted by four ballast tanks located beneath the floor. These were filled with water to allow the dock to sink to a level to give enough depth for vessels to enter and then replaced by compressed air to lift the whole building above the water level by about 6 inches. To flood the dock again, the air is replaced with water to a depth of 3.2 metres, sufficient to float vessels of up to 1200 tons in and out.

Work then started immediately and caught us a bit on the hop. Three of the men had started sealing all apertures with soft board and gaffer tape - windows, air vents, pigeon boxes, everything was being sealed in preparation for the blasting. We were leaving to return to England but we had to quickly get our stuff together and get off the boat before we were sealed up inside ourselves! The entire operation here was run by just seven staff, which included the three brothers Den Breejen. We finalised the details of the work with Dijk, who seemed to be the head man, loaded our bags into the car, and headed back to the Hook for the evening ferry back to Harwich. Half way there I had a sudden thought.

"Could you just check that my wallet is in the glove box please Mike?"

It wasn't and we searched the car inside out. We stopped in a layby and went through the bags. Bugger! What the hell had I done with it? The only possible answer was that I had left it on the boat. We couldn't carry on to the ferry without it so the only alternative was to turn around and go back. There was still time - just, but we wouldn't be able to hang about. In the event I suppose I shouldn't have been that surprised when Broderick Crawford, the Mountie on the Electra Glide, waltzed past with a wave of the arm and signalled for me to follow him. That's all we needed, and as if he'd known about our urgency, he led us down various side-roads and back streets before stopping in a pleasant grove miles from the motorway. I was now passportless - and lost. Kojak dismounted his steed and strolled across to where we were sitting, side window lowered, and lifted his visor.

"Goot effening sir. Passport please."

"Ah - well that's the point. You see we were in rather a hurry to get back to my boat which is in Dordrecht as we are booked on the ten o'clock ferry to England and I think I have left my passport on the boat."

"Driving Licence."

Ah - yes - driving licence - well that is in the same wallet as my passport which as I explained I have left on my boat in Dordrecht."

"ID Card."

Ah - ID card - well I am sorry to say that the good old British government, in the face of some opposition from the liberal left, have yet to introduce ID cards in Britain and as I said all my papers are in the same wallet as my passport which is on the boat and which we are in rather a hurry to find."

"So you haff no means of identification." His English was annoyingly good for a bone-head motorbike cop. I looked blank.

"Then I haff to arrest you for being in our Country with no means of identification. It is a criminal offence."

59

Our hopes of catching that ferry were diminishing by the second.

He paused to allow sufficient time for his threat to make a satisfying impact - satisfying to him and his ego anyway although it hadn't done a lot for our sense of humour.

"As you have to go to Enklant," he said slowly, "and as you must have a passport to go to Enklantd..." - he was grinning smugly now as I wondered briefly what the food was like in Dutch jails -"then I will let you go but you must drive more schlowly. Do you understant?"

I certainly did understand and almost thanked him.

"The problem now is that I don't know the way back to the motorway. Could you possibly give me directions please?" I crawled, adding for good measure, "Officer."

"No problem - follow me," he beamed, kicking the Electra Glide into life.

Then he disappeared in a cloud of dust before I even had the chance to turn the ignition. Bastard!

By the time we got back to the yard they had closed, and for a moment I thought I might have to call Dijk to get him back and let us in. Luckily however the gate was unlocked - I think a couple of the lads lived on the premises - and so we were able to get into the dock. There was a ladder up against the side of the boat and we climbed aboard. The next problem of course was that everything had been sealed up and we had to cut away with a penknife at one of the wheelhouse doors so that I could get inside. Once in the saloon I saw it - plain as day sitting on the coffee table - my wallet containing passport, driving licence and credit cards. I phoned the yard the next day to explain what we had done and apologised for messing up their handiwork. Dijk said that it would not be a problem but I had a lingering worry that the re-seal job would never be as good as the original. As it happened I was right about that.

We made it to the ferry with about half an hour to spare and collapsed exhausted in the bar.

One more day in the life.....

We disembarked at Harwich early the next morning. The immigration officer checked our passports and told me that his "mate" from HMRC would like a word. When we arrived at the

Customs shed I got the once over and a grilling as to where we'd been, why, how long for etc. They had a pretty careful search inside and outside over and under the car, and then, just as I was thinking about the snap of the rubberglove, almost reluctantly sent us on our way.

"What was all that about?" I asked Mike.

"Well think about it," he said, leafing through my passport. "You've got stamps in here from the last few years for Malaysia, India, Thailand, Vietnam, Cambodia, Australia, Hong Kong, Singapore. Now we've just been to Holland and back in a day. Don't you think that might make them a bit suspicious?"

"Yeah - suppose so," I had to admit, "hadn't thought of that. Just as well they didn't look in there then."

I opened the small compartment next to the gear lever where I'd put the two little funny fags I'd bought for 2 Euros in the coffee shop at Dordrecht - medicinal purposes of course!

"Christ," said Mike, "if they'd found them they would have torn the bloody car apart."

One of these days I'll learn to grow up and become sensible - maybe.

Actually in retrospect I'm not so sure I should have included that in a book. I have just seen that CJ whatsisname from the Eggheads programme, has been arrested because of something he'd written in his autobiography. Mind you that was a bit more serious. He had admitted that he pushed a mugger into a canal in Amsterdam and wrote that for all he knew he had probably drowned. Not quite the same as being in possession of a couple of dodgy cigarettes.

Over the winter I began to get increasingly worried about Otto. I had asked him to do a few small jobs and it was becoming more and more apparent that he hadn't got much idea of what he was doing. The only thing he seemed any good at was trying to extort money from me. I won't elaborate - he had done a lot of work for Michael Mortimer who didn't have a bad word to say about him but I came to the conclusion that he was a bit of a conman - exploitative, unreliable and incompetent. This was further borne out when I went back to Den Breejen. It was fairly obvious that they thought the same and told me so, which didn't exactly do a lot for my confidence. In the end I refused to pay his final bill which was totally exhorbitant and unjustified, and we finally settled the matter, not without acrimony on both sides, and I begrudgingly paid him half. I felt that you couldn't trust him any further than you could lower him down a short well.

Ah well - you win some and you lose some - and as my friend Fred Tutt would say -" it's all swings and roundabouts. It's just that sometimes there are more bloody roundabouts than there are swings!"

I drove back to Dordrecht with Rob at the end of May. Dijk shook hands but wasn't over-welcoming. He threw me the keys and said something like" it's outside", then left us to it while he concentrated on the more important matters in hand. I hadn't expected a champagne reception - this was a working shipyard after all and my 14000 Euro job was a mere piss in the ocean (if you'll pardon the pun) to him. I did think he might have taken a few minutes to actually show us to the boat, but "dat ist het leven" as they say in Dordrecht, or c'est la vie, as we say in Salisbury.

After clambering up and down bare steel stairways and dodging around sheets of plating, girders and huge tins of paint and tar, we made our way to the dock, where there was another 1000 tonner, the Majestic, undergoing the treatment. Then through a door into the open air and - where was Saul Trader? Immediately alongside the wall there was another commercial and astern of that was the steel structure that housed the mechanism for raising and lowering the dock. But Saul Trader was nowhere to be seen.

While we were standing there looking dim, one of the lads came by and I asked him where they had put it. He pointed to the other side of the machinery block.

Don't look behind you - Elionie entering the dry-dock

Rob in socialise mode on board Saul Trader with Berry and Marion

"Over there," he said and disappeared.

Getting "over there" was no mean feat either. First we had to climb 10 feet down a vertical ladder, then negotiate our way around the sides of the building on a ledge about 18 inches wide, and 15 feet above the water level. Finally at the outer corner we saw Saul Trader, moored alongside the building, 10 feet below! There were no ladders and the only way to get aboard was to jump. We didn't have Scragg with us this time to help on his way with a push, so as the youngest in the party it was down to me. The worst that could happen was to break both legs, or a neck perhaps, but I was definitely not going back to Dijk to borrow a ladder. Jumping, after all, was just a leap of faith. When I was young I'd think nothing of jumping from trees with pockets full of scrumped apples, but nowadays, apart from the obvious risk of damage to brittle bones, I seemed to get a peculiar sort of rush of blood to the head when descending more than about six feet through gravity, which was a little disconcerting.

However there was no time to go into the medical possibilities, a jump had to be made. I crouched down and sat on the edge of the walkway, hoping somehow that this might lessen the drop. I was aiming for the foredeck of Saul Trader - a foredeck that I must say looked very smart in its fresh coat of semi-matt oxide paint and that suddenly, after a short lift from the elbows and a quick push off came rushing towards me. I landed - not particularly elegantly, but more or less with orthopaedic accoutrements intact. I was looking for some way of getting Rob down when I heard a thud, followed by an aw shit, and there he was on the deck, rolled on to his back, legs pointing upwards,

"I hope you haven't damaged the paintwork," I said sympathetically.

When he'd picked himself up and dusted himself down and remarked that the drop was a bit further than he thought it was, we looked over the paint job.

We had to admit that Den Breejen had done a fantastic job and the boat looked like new.

Then we unlocked the wheelhouse and stepped inside and ....Oh my God!

Everything, but everything, was covered in a layer of dust an eighth of an inch thick. It was as though someone had laid a coir mat over the whole of the inside. It was all over the floors, in the beds, the shelves, the sinks, the toilets, the instrument panels and even inside the books. It was quite soul destroying to see and if I'd have been a girl I would have burst into tears. In lieu of that, however, we were men, and we just stared at it all in utter disbelief. One thing was certain, we wouldn't be able to stay on the boat tonight or for that matter for several more nights ahead.

I went to see Dijk to see what could be done and he agreed to lend us a couple of industrial hoovers and one of his men, Mutt, and we set to work with a will. Mutt and Rob were fantastic and methodically cleaned out every nook and cranny. At least it was dry dust and swept cleanly into the machines. It was difficult to know where to start but I tackled the wheelhouse with the boat's hoover while Rob and Mutt started to clear the two forward cabins. We filled the large machines four times each in the first day and emptied what seemed like a ton of dust.

Fortunately, Rob had a friend who lived on the outskirts of Dordrecht, and Berry kindly offered us the use of a room at his place to sleep. Berry was a bit of a musician and had a small studio set up in his house, with guitars, amplifiers and an electronic drum machine. We had a great evening with Berry playing guitar, Rob on the kazoo and me on the drums - just what we needed to take our minds off the enormous task of cleaning up the boat. Berry's musical tastes weren't at all bad for a Dutchman, his pièce de résistance being a folksong that I knew from the 60's, "In the early Morning Rain". The lyrics seemed ominously appropriate,

*"In the early morning rain with a dollar in my hand
And an aching in my heart, and my pockets full of sand."*

Well God knows - it wasn't just our bloody pockets, we had sand every bloody where!

Wasn't it Kenneth Williams in Carry on Camel who came out with the line "sand in our hair, sand in our sandals, sand in our sandwiches!"

I learned something else too. I knew that the song was written and recorded by Gordon Lightfoot and I had never heard any other versions of it. Berry insisted that he had a version by Bob Dylan and sure enough, there it was as plain as day - on the "Self Portrait" album. We then did a bit more research on the ethereal Encyclopedia Brittanica, otherwise known as the Worldwide Web, and discovered that it had also been recorded by Elvis Presley, Peter Paul and Mary, and even Paul Weller. You learn something every day.

Berry and his wife Marion looked after us royally for the three days it took to make Saul Trader habitable again with some great food and interesting musical interludes.

By pure chance, the Dordt in Stoom steam festival was taking place that very weekend. This was the wonderful extravaganza of all things steam - boats, trains and traction engines - that takes place every two years around the old dock area of Dordrecht. We had visited in 2004, when a drunken Dutchman had accosted us on the train and insisted on feeding us with Calvados straight from the bottle by way of thanks for saving his Country from the Germans in World War ll.

Rob had never been and I must say that I needed no persuasion at all about seeing it all again. On the Friday evening all the participating vessels, large and small, and some that aren't participating, steam up and down the Beneden Merwede, generally showing off and blowing their whistles. There are tugs and passenger launches, paddle-steamers and tiny camping skiffs with tan sails. There doesn't seem to be any rule of the road - you just go where you please, and all this whilst the regular commercial tonnage ploughs through the melee. No closing the road here and no exhibitionist police outriders flying all over the place. This is Holland, and on this particular evening at least, anything goes. I was tempted to take Saul Trader out into the fray with its shiny new paintwork, but thought better of it. I'm not even sure whether it was allowed. I suppose they couldn't just let any old Tom

Dijk and Harry out there or it would turn into a complete free-for-all.

Joe Parfitt came up with Door from Migennes and we all watched the fun from the fifth floor apartment that belonged to a friend of Berry, which gave us a fantastic view across the river towards the lights of Rotterdam that glinted in the distance. At one point a huge fire-fighting barge went past, drenching everything in sight with its massive water cannons, and I think I saw Joe almost break into a smile.

On the Saturday we did the circular trip which involved a leisurely cruise upstream on the steam launch "Animathor" with morning coffee, a visit to the vast model exhibition, a ride behind a magnificently restored German Pacific steam locomotive back to Dordrecht Central station, followed by a bouncy trip on a vintage DAF autobus - and all this for just 8 Euros each. We didn't see our friend with the Calvados luckily, but amazingly we got talking to a couple sitting opposite us on the train who it transpired, came from Hastings. As a boy the husband had lived next door to a good friend of mine and indeed we had all played together in his back garden many years ago. Small World, we often say, but that is not quite correct. In fact it's a very big World and someone once devised an elaborate theory as to why we quite often bumped into someone with a connection to our past in the most unexpected of circumstances. Basically the theory was that during our three score and ten years we made so many millions of tenuous contacts that by the law of probabilities there was every chance that we would come into contact with people who knew someone we once knew, lived somewhere close to where we once lived, or went to school or worked somewhere that we once did. So the fact that I had met someone in Phnom Phen who was related to the local butcher in Hollington where my mother bought her meat should actually be no surprise at all, if you follow the thinking. Nevertheless it is still a humanly touching experience, so sod the theorists.

On the way back to the boat we were completely drenched through by a sudden hailstorm that sent us diving for cover to avoid being knocked out by hailstones literally the size of golf balls. Luckily the nearest cover was our favourite little dockside bar.

While we were in Holland it seemed rude not spend a few weeks cruising some of the wondrous waterways that criss-cross the landscape like country lanes. Amazingly there are just over 3500 kilometres of navigable waterway in Holland compared with 8500 in France.

The number of locks - just 186 in Holland, France boasts over 2000 - ideal cruising ground for the not-so-active, or the just plain lazy!

We changed the oil and filters, something I tried to do at least every 250 hours, and by way of a thank you for their hospitality, we took Berry and Marion with us on the first day from Dordrecht to Alphen aan den Rhin, and Rob treated us to one of his barbecue lunches. We passed the yard where Otto had suggested we could be lifted out and it was painfully obvious that this was never going to be feasible. Apart from the absence of anything like a big enough crane, there wasn't an inch of spare ground amongst all the steel motor cruisers. Otto was not around. He had taken his family on a cruise - probably funded by yours truly!

Alphen aan den Rhin is no longer actually on the Rhin. Due to frequent flooding of the town a dyke was constructed in the early part of the 12th Century which diverted the Rhine and immediately solved the flooding problem. I think Upton on Severn could have used that information, although they have since installed protective barriers which I believe has alleviated most of the flooding. The river through Alphen is known as the Oude Rhin and runs through the centre of the town, bordered by attractive walkways, cafes, shops and apartments.

We sat in the sunshine in a café on the Heerlijk Terras beside the Alphensebrug, where a "Diverse Lunch" was advertised on an "A" board at 8 Euros. What exactly a diverse lunch consisted of we didn't find out - maybe they had topless waitresses! We contented ourselves with latte and pastries and watched as the 85 metre bulk carrier Harmonie, squeezed its 9 metre beam through the tiny bridge opening with inches to spare, closely followed by two small open power boats and a canoe. That sort of summed up Dutch waterways - there seemed to be room for everyone, young and old, large and small.

The following morning we said goodbye to Berry and Marion who left to catch a train back to Dordrecht, and turned right on to the Heimanswetering to head for the wide open expanse of the Braassemermeer, a 1000 acre lake. We tied up at a marina on the western side astern of Rob's friend Michael Mortimer with his lovely golden retriever Daisy, on his equally lovely Super van Kraft motor yacht "Gypsy". Sitting outside in the warm evening June sunshine with a cool Hoegaarden topped with a thin slice of citron, it was difficult to imagine that the lake is a popular location for the sport of Ijszeilvereniging - and I'm sure you would do too if you knew what it was. Basically it's sailing on ice. A single sail is attached to a sort of sledge with a keel and outriggers on each side for balance. The sail is set and they speed off over the frozen lake. Apparently they can reach speeds of up to 100 kph and one has even been recorded at 170 kph. What happens if you capsize I dread to think! Let go of everything and hope for the best I suppose. There are strict rules as to the designs and to determine who gives way to whom. At closing speeds of 200kph it must be quite difficult to know which side to go and when - you can't really just shout "starboard" and expect the other sledge to get out of your way.

From the Braassemermeer we headed north through the channel known as the Oude Wetering before turning left and heading back to Leiden, where we were going to meet up again with Mike and Sue. It was good to have Rob around and once he got used to the idea of pushing the Morse throttle lever forward to go ahead and back to go astern, he was fine.

Tight squeeze - Alpen an Der Rhin

On the way we passed through the Kaags, a small lake system just north of Leiden, and tied for the night on a short pontoon at Warmond. We had tried to moor on a convenient wall with mooring rings but ten minutes after we had finished securing and two minutes before we were due to crack open the first beer of the day, two laid-back members of the Politie arrived in a Volkswagen Beetle and casually strolled over to tell us politely to bugger off. They reminded me of the TV sketches that Harry Enfield and Paul Whitehouse used to do as the two Dutch policemen, "Ve vere schitting by ze Zeider Zee..." There were very few places to stop - there were boats everywhere, but they did tell us that we could use a pontoon on the opposite bank. It was about fifteen metres too short but it served and we found a very attractive little bar with a very jovial crowd who made us more than welcome. The Kaag Lakes are a popular area for boating, and fishing, with low grassy areas and grazing cattle where the banks are dotted with windmills and beautiful little waterside homes - exactly how you think of Holland, apart from the absence of tulips, although on reflection that may have been due to the Season. Many of these immaculate dwellings had their own small mooring with a smart launch moored at the bottom of the garden. In places it reminded me very much of some areas of the Norfolk Broads, particularly around Wroxham, which was where Mike and Sue were now living. At Kaag we took on 500 litres of diesel at the buttock-clenching price of 1.30 Euros per litre.

We found a nice convenient mooring close to the centre of Leiden and walked to the station to meet them. It was always good to have them on the boat. I had known Mike for almost fifty years and although we might go for a year or eighteen months without any contact, I would suddenly get a call out of the blue from him in Bombay or Hong Kong or some other far-flung outpost - wherever he happened to be in the execution of his duties as a professional mariner. It was a friendship that had endured in spite of the thousands of miles and many years between meet-ups. Mike and Sue had been married for more than forty years. They had met when Mike was a young Cadet on the P&O liner "Chusan", and Sue was on a cruise. Mike had spent 40 odd years at sea in one capacity or another. He had gained his Master's Certificate with the Merchant Navy and had spells on ocean-going survey ships, oil-rig support vessels in the North Sea and the Baltic, and even for a couple of years as mate on the Irish sail training brig, the Asgard. He also spent fifteen years as a Lieutenant Commander in the Sultan of Oman's Navy and had been an advisor during the multi-million dollar construction in Italy of His Majesty the Sultan's royal dhow. Needless to say, all this varied experience had left Mike with more than his fair share of stories.

Sue had lived there with him in Oman where she had worked for a local company. She also had a soft spot for stray dogs and at one time I think she had six or seven adoptees. She even brought some of them back to England when they returned to live in Norfolk. There had been a number of wives and/or girlfriends with us on Saul Trader, and I must say that some of them rather got under my skin after a while. I suppose I'm not the most tolerant (*understatement - Ed)* and I did sometimes get a bit ratty. The bossy ones, the fussy ones and the stupid ones eventually over-tried my patience which now and again led to a bit of minor acrimony - well minor in my estimation if not in theirs. But Suzy was brilliant. She never complained about anything, never tried to tell me which side to pass buoys, always took an interest in what was going on, cooked some very tasty meals and usually ended up by completely clearing out all the galley cupboards, tutting to herself and chucking away tins and jars which I had been lovingly saving for years. She even ditched a can of beans which was only seven years past its sell-by date!

We didn't really have a plan. I think at the time the plan was that there was no plan, but we headed north in the general direction of Amsterdam. We squeezed into a mooring that was about two inches longer than the boat in between two very expensive looking motor yachts at Ouderkerk aan de Amstel. Thanks to the bow-thruster I made it look as though I could put the boat on a sixpence. This was true as long as I could find a sixpence big enough. One thing I had learnt though was not to get too cocky because very soon you would meet your comeuppance if you weren't very careful.

As a tyre fitter in Salisbury once told me when I enquired as to the state of business.

"Not too bad - don't speak too soon though fall flat on its face else."

A prophecy almost fulfilled the following day on the approach to Amsterdam. This was a sort of back-door route through the southern suburbs on the Amstel. There were a lot of wonderful little split bridges, some of which carried trams, that would rise up like a guard of honour at a wedding to let you pass. One of these was situated just before a blind left hand bend and when the bridge raised I started forward anticipating the green light which never came. Instead a tug towing four dumb barges filled with rubbish came hurtling round the turn from the opposite direction flat out. I had to apply anchors in emergency mode sending the rev counter off the clock and clouds of black smoke into the ether.

Always expect the unexpected! (*and never make assumptions - Ed*).

We passed a sign that announced "Heineken Experience" but we didn't succumb. Had it said "Hook Norton Experience" or "Timothy Taylor's Landlord Experience" it may have been tempting, but the lagers - well, once you'd experienced one you'd experienced them all.

After a careful bit of navigating with the aid of the Karte we skirted the futuristic edifice of the Nemo Science Museum before turning left in to the entrance of the Oosterdok. A friendly resident boater let us moor alongside him for the bargain price of a couple of bottles of wine and we stayed for two nights. The Oosterdok is very convenient for the centre of Amsterdam and we took the opportunity to stroll around and take in the ambience. We window-shopped along the Molensteeg with its scarlet neon-lit temptations which led into the open air square by the Oude Kerk. The Dutch have adopted a liberal and almost anything-goes policy, summed up satirically by Paul Whitehouse as the laid-back Amsterdam policeman with ginger moustache, Captain Stefan Van der Graaf Haas, when he says smirking.

"We used to have a big problem wiz burglary here but ve haff a vay to tackle it and since we legalise burglary it is no longer a problem."

Beneath its liberal façade, Amsterdam harbours a dangerous and insidious underworld. The sex trade is simply a tourist lure run by foreign infiltrators and gangsters. Very few, if any of the girls are Dutch, most coming from Hungary and other parts of Eastern Europe. It's a dark and sinister business riddled with all types of crime and best avoided. We drew the line at the Sexmuseum - over-rated as someone once said, although on reflection I suppose it's been around long enough to warrant having a museum.

Sex education class -

The teacher says, "There are 99 known sexual positions, the first of these ...."

"100," shouts young Willy from the back of the class.

Unperturbed, the teacher starts again.

"There are 99 known sexual positions, the first of these ...."

"100," repeats Willy.

The teacher clears his throat.

"If you will let me finish. There are 99 known sexual positions, the first of these being the missionary position.

"A hundred and one!" exclaims Willy to raucous laughter from the class. I don't know whether there were examples of all 100 on display in the museum.

Our sort of bar - Dordrecht

Dordt in Stoom

This one even raised a smile from Jo

Back in the 'narrows'

Amsterdam

Chapter 5   More Dutch Delights

Our exit from the Oosterdock took us under the entire width of Amsterdam Central Station into the vast dock area known as the Hout Haven that serves the Nordzeekanal and provides passenger facilities large enough for the biggest ocean liners. There are many things to see here but this is no place for sightseeing. Vessels appear from right and left from smaller canals and criss-cross from one side to the other and concentration is essential. It is a bit like driving around Piccadilly Circus. We had to cross to the far side and then find the entrance to our intended route, the Noordhollandsche Kanaal, not as easy as one might think. To start with there were several "entrances", and it was difficult to know quite which one to take. There were no twee little finger posts here, like you get at some of the junctions on the English canals. There was basically a choice of three. The one to the right led into a dead end and the one to the left seemed to take you around a loop which ended up back in the Hout Haven. We decided to try the middle one and our decision was vindicated when on the approach we spotted a lock some hundred yards ahead with twinkly red and green lights, indicating that the lock was being prepared. Not surprisingly, it wasn't for us that it was being prepared, but a medium-size commercial that Mike announced was coming up astern. We let him overtake and cautiously waited until he'd settled his bum in the lock before slowly going in behind. Directly after leaving the lock our companion turned off into a small harbour on the left and we were on our own once again.

The canal narrowed quite considerably as we got nearer to Monnickerdam. We passed through some more lifting bridges with inches to spare and a small lock with a rise of just a metre, before a sharp right turn. Monnickerdam was full of small boats moored on short pontoons on both sides of the channel. We passed several busy shipyards and alongside one of them a newly completed super-yacht of Roman Abramovich proportions - well on reflection maybe a bit small for him, more a Timothy West perhaps. God knows the damage and chaos that he could reek at the wheel of one of these!

I would implore any aspiring canal-boater who has seen any of this pompous buffoon's TV documentaries to totally disregard anything they may have seen Mr West advocate as the norm. The canals are not a glorified dodgem track and it is not accepted practice to go around crashing into other boats willy nilly and anyone doing so might well end up with a bloody nose. He had crashed stem to stem into my narrowboat some years ago while it was moored breasted up on the outside of another boat at Cropredy during the Fairport festival weekend. I wasn't there at the time but other people who witnessed it said that he was looking at his guide book at the time and not where he was going and the impact was so great that it sent him veering off into the opposite bank and almost into one of the gardens. They suggested to his wife, Prunella, who had come out on to the well deck to see what was going on, that they should leave a contact number in case any damage had been done. When she told Mr West he just dismissed it with a wave of his hand. Arrogant and irresponsible and a sad example to set other boaters. He says that canal boating is "a contact sport!" I would suggest to him that the only contact that is acceptable is in the social sense. If he wants to drive headlong into walls and bridges that's up to him although it won't do a lot of good to the already ailing infrastructure. I once locked through a flight with a retired working boatman, the iconic Arthur Bray, and although he didn't exactly hang around, he steered his boat with immaculate precision and never once collided with, or even scraped, the lock walls or the gates. A true gentleman of the cut.

There are several "personalities" who own narrowboats on the cut. Timothy Spall's travels were well documented on TV and Harrison Ford has been known to have several narrowboat holidays. A friend of mine encountered Mr Spall in Limehouse Basin one evening and as he walked past nodded and said, "Good evening."

Mr Spall looked up from his book and said disdainfully,

"Do I know you?"

Now anyone with any knowledge of the lore of the cut, even in these modern times, appreciates the fact that boaters acknowledge each other and sometimes even stop to chat. Mr Spall had obviously not read that part of the script. I told Richard he should have replied.

"No - and I don't know you either, but it is the custom to say hello to people on the cut."

I have had contact with David Suchet in the past - a perfect gentleman with a love and respect for the English canals, who has owned several boats over the years, and who has been a staunch supporter of many canal restoration projects. I spoke to him once about my Large Woolwich working boat, the Birmingham. He was absolutely charming and told me that if I ever saw him on his boat, to be sure to knock and come in for a cup of tea. Unfortunately I never did get the opportunity which was a shame - but what a difference. A humble and considerate man who unlike Mr West did not wander around oblivious to his surroundings and to the lore of the cut.

The Spalls and Wests of this world may well have been very good actors but no need to be quite so up their own bottoms! Personally I think the BBC are guilty of association for showing such ridiculous crap and it should be banned. After all, just think of some of the innocuous things they have banned over the years - George Formby's "When I'm Cleaning Windows", The Kinks' "Lola", the Sex Pistols "God Save the Queen", Mott the Hoople's "All the Young Dudes", and even Lonnie Donegan's "Diggin my Potatoes!". What's more likely to do irreparable damage to the fabric of society I ask? Lonnie Donegan or Timothy bloody West! (*have you finished now ? - Ed*)

At Monnickerdam the canal opens into the inland sea known as the Gouwzee which to the North becomes the Markermeer. This in turn becomes the Ijsselmeer which leads through locks beneath the 32 kilometre long Waddensee causeway, the Afsluitdijk (pronounced phlegm!) in to the North Sea. We were not going that far, however, which was just as well as there was a thick fog which had narrowed visibility down to a few hundred yards. What's more, we didn't have proper charts and had to rely on the Dutch canal map for navigation. Our "landfall" was Edam, some eight or so kilometres to the North, and after all, we had an old sea-dog on board in the form of Mike, who got out the parallel rule and worked out a rudimentary course.

Rob went for'ard to act as lookout and we motored very slowly out of the confines of the canal as the channel widened under the road bridge that carries the N247 into the Monnickerdamgat and after another three kilometres we were in the Gouwzee. Rob peered into the gloom and suddenly called out.

"Vessel on the port bow - difficult to make out. It's either moving very slowly or anchored."

A few minutes later Mike picked it out with the binoculars and confirmed that it was showing a black shape on the forestay, indicating that it was anchored. As we got nearer the shape appeared as a ghostly apparition and we could make out masts and leeboards. There were in fact two large sailing barges anchored alongside each other and we passed them about 100 yards away. I did wonder whether they were playing safe by anchoring and that maybe we should be doing likewise, but while I was thinking Mike pointed out the headland just visible on our left where we would be altering course to port to steer 045° which would take us clear of the causeway that stuck out three kilometres to the north of the small island of Marken. Rob pulled his cap down over his forehead and doggedly surveyed the scene. I remembered days on the old Arcadia when we would put a Seacunny right up on the bow, usually clad in a duffle coat with the hood pulled up, who would ring a bell every two minutes as we silently glided into the fog, as a warning to other vessels of our presence. It always struck me as a rather primitive way to navigate a 30,000 ton ship, especially in crowded waters like the English Channel!

After six kilometres on this heading the fog had virtually cleared, and we made another alteration after Mike had taken a couple of bearings with the hand-held compass that put us about a kilometre off the headland north of Volendam. Rob was relieved of lookout duties and took the helm while I made some coffee and sarnies and we headed on 350° towards the tiny entrance of the canal that led to the town of Edam.

We were soon back in the fascinating network of narrow Dutch backwater canals with quaint lift bridges and minimal clearances. After passing a large basin known as the Oorgat (we had come across this word before -"gat"- and according to Google translate it means literally "hole", so I suppose this was a sort of mooring hole called Oor?) We negotiated a small lock before tying up in another small basin next to a lovely ornate little lift bridge, the Kettingbrug. From here it was a short walk into the town where we found a bar, surprise surprise, and took in the ale, and the ambience. While we were there a strange sort of marching jazz band appeared, led by two children carrying two round cheeses on a sort of stretcher with handles. They were all dressed rather like English Morris dancers, apart from the lack of bells and the addition of clogs, (*don't forget the Lancashire clog-dancers, Ed*) with white shirts and trousers, straw boaters with colourful bands and neckerchiefs. A small procession had gathered behind them and we, as good conforming tourists, joined in behind. We were all going to a traditional cheese market, where there were stalls selling all kinds of cheeses wrapped in colourful skins and laid out on the ground, big ones and small ones and some as big as your head, and ladies going amongst the crowds with sample tasters - of the cheese that is and not the ladies.

All this fun and jocularity made us rather hungry and we found a nearby restaurant that provided some interesting fare and some extremely edible puddings. Apparently these desserts were a bit of a speciality of the restaurant "Het Genheim". It was all a bit haut cuisiney for me but very tasty nonetheless and the cheesecakey thing with raspberries and blueberries topped with whipped cream rather sealed it.

I'm sorry if I'm getting boring, but I feel another anecdote coming on here on the subject of haut cuisine.

A friend of ours, known as Buzzard who hailed from Bolton and who was rather partial to good old fashioned English fare, like gut-buster breakfasts with black (and white) pudding, was taken by his wife to a gourmet restaurant in Warwick. They had waited for twenty five minutes after ordering, when the young lady waitress brought two ultra large plates each with a tiny dollop of something in the middle surrounded by some powdery stuff and a bit of what looked like raspberry juice.

"Excuse me dear," said Buzzard, "what's this?"

"That's your appetiser, sir," the young lady replied.

"Well it's bloody well worked - now please bring me my dinner will you," said Buzzard, handing back the plate.

On the way out of Edam we were held at the first tiny lift bridge. There were boats on both sides of the canal and just enough room for us to squeeze past. There was a small vintage tug on the right just before the bridge and we nestled gently alongside, taking care not to do any damage to the immaculate paintwork. There was someone working in the engine room and he came out and kindly took a rope. As soon as we had secured, Rob's nose was in the engine hatch and the owner started to launch into a detailed explanation of the vital statistics of his wondrous engine. He was like a tour guide, spieling off fact after fact which meant little to me but a bit more to Rob. I could see he was champing at the bit to get his five eggs in about his own vintage "lump" but there was no way that Gunter was going to give him a chance. He rarely stopped for breath as he gabbled on about horse power and gear boxes and compression ratios and all sorts of other mystical things. The engine was a 2 cylinder 2 stroke Kromhout from the 1950's, and I could tell he was just dying for someone to ask him to start it up.

"Do you think you could you start it up for us?" I asked him.

He skipped around like a featherweight boxer, opening this valve and that, pumping something else, adjusting various other bits this way and that, before giving the motor a friendly pat, and then, giving us a look of "wait for it", he pushed the starter. A couple of coughs and a splutter, a wheeze and a bang, and the whole thing began to shake and shudder, rocking the little tug from side to side as the two cylinders started to pump up and down, levers clicked to and fro and gauges flickered, until it all settled into a gentle ticking motion with a soporific bass drum beat.

Phil Trotter was a bit of a genius with old engines and he had restored several Kelvin K3's, rescued from a lifetime of work in lighthouses apparently powering fog horns. They were a bit on the large side for narrowboats - it was a bit like putting a cathedral organ into a country chapel but Phil had installed one in his Northwich replica narrowboat "Alnwick." He told me that one Sunday morning he had cast off from the Cape of Good Hope at six o'clock and gently passed a moored boat with the engine on tickover and doing about 10 revs a minute, when a bloke stuck his head out of the hatch and told him.

"I've got a bone to pick with you, young man."

He must have been a bit short-sighted!

"My wife's just had her first orgasm in fifteen years listening to your bloody engine."

I 'ad a single Bolinder and it was a fine machine
It used to goo like 'ell in the night when all its parts were clean
I fired 'er up one morning at the bottom of Itchington Ten
I was 'alf way down the Bascote pound before it fired again
And it'd burn a gallon a stroke
Titty fa-la titty fa-lay
Yer could see sod all for smoke
Titty fa-la titty fa-lay
I wound her up full blast, the motor went so fast
It pulled out the butty's mast
Titty fa-la titty fa-lay
Tra, la, la-la- la- la - smacking it into the cut

Thanks to David Blagrove (to be sung to the beat of a single Bolinder)

At last the bridge was raised and we let go and said our farewells to Gunter, the steady beat of the engine slowly fading into the distance as we inched through the gap and passed a wonderful little village boatyard that had its own slip where small boats could be winched out of the water on cradles to await attention. It looked like something out of a 1950's working museum!

Each year for the past five or so I have told myself that it's time to sell the boat. I'm getting too old and the boat is getting more like hard work, but I'm still here and writing about Holland has made me think about going back. Saul Trader is way down south at the moment of writing - in Toulouse in fact, but maybe, just maybe, I'll start making plans to bring it north again and spend another summer in the wonderland of the Dutch canals. My appetite has been re-whetted!

After several more lift bridges we had reluctantly left Edam behind for open country. There was a fixed bridge on our route which according to the karte had a height clearance of 3.6 metres. Our height was 3.6 metres so, in the absence of any fat ladies it could mean having to lower the wheelhouse. We hadn't had to do this for four or five years. I think the last time was when we were stuck in Witmarsum on a tiny ditch of a canal between Harlingen and Bolsward in Friesland. We had plenty of hands so the exercise shouldn't pose a big problem but as it turned out we didn't need to bother. We approached the bridge very slowly and decided that with the heating chimney down we would just about make it - and just about we did, with about an inch to spare. We followed the canal through Purmerend and then re-joined the Noordhollandische canal as far as West Graftdijk, where we turned south to skirt another inland lake, the Alkmaardermeer. At Wormerveer we were held at a railway lift bridge where we had to telephone to check in and ask for clearance. We waited as three double deck regional expresses passed before the cantilever bridge opened and the green light gave us the right of way. I don't really know why, but I am always wary of these railway crossings. They are obviously fail-safe and no more dangerous than level crossings on roads, but there's just something about them that makes me slightly nervous, especially, as with this one, when they are controlled from afar. Safely through, we breathed a sigh of relief and continued on the Vaardijk canal to its junction with the M3 motorway, or the Nordzeekanaal as it's known in Holland.

This is a junction which definitely should have traffic lights. It's a case of look left, look right, look left again, then wait as another three or four leviathans steam past. This is the canal that connects Amsterdam with the North Sea and carries very large and very fast ships - as large as 90,000 tons in fact - the sort of ships you don't want to upset! We turned right and tucked in as near to the side as we could, while two or three vessels swept past in mid-channel on their way to the locks at Ijmuiden which would lower them into the North Sea.

Our next turn was only just over a kilometre away but the tricky bit was that it was a left turn which meant that we had to cross the channel from right to left. With 500 metres or so to go, we had three vessels coming towards us and nothing, for the moment, astern. I thought we could get to the opposite side in front of the oncoming ships and then creep up close to the bank and show our blue board, to let them know that we would pass starboard to starboard. But the authority, in this case Lt Commander Mike wouldn't hear of it. With fifty years of sea-going experience behind him, albeit not involving the blue board rule, I didn't feel like disagreeing with him, so we waited patiently as all three sped past before making a dash to the entrance of the much quieter Zijkanaal which would take us to our day's destination at the medieval city of Haarlem, where we found a good mooring on the wall in the centre of the town, opposite the imposing landmark of the Adriaan windmill.

By pure coincidence we happened to moor about ten paces away from the entrance to a rather lively bar. By another coincidence the 2010 World Cup was about to start and the bar was showing the opening game, South Africa against Mexico. Rob and I retired to the bar and Mike and Suzy went out to explore the town. Mike was not really into football. He professed to be a fan of West Ham United but this was put in some doubt many years ago when he'd got married at 3 o'clock on the very day that West Ham were playing in the FA Cup Final at Wembley. Surely any "proper" self-respecting football fan would have done the decent thing - and cancelled the wedding.

The game was dominated by the Mexicans, but it was South Africa who scored first, early in the second half, with a brilliant goal by Tshabalala and the Dutch, most of whom were supporting South Africa for obvious reasons, went completely beserk. They sang their heads off for twenty five minutes before the Mexico captain, Rafael Marquez, brought them back to earth with a thump - a thump from close range that gave them a well-deserved draw.

The following evening it was the turn of Fabio Capello's England to let everybody down. We took our seats within range of the bar and the TV screen ten minutes before the kick off and the place was soon packed with Dutchmen, eager to witness another English embarrassment. Rob insisted on singing God Save the Queen very loudly, not a particularly sensible thing to do in a bar half full of Americans, especially as his rendering was sung more to the tune of Old Man River! Anyone looking forward to a complete English humiliation was almost - almost - disappointed when England scored first with a goal from Steven Gerrard after just four minutes, but true-to-form, our gallant boys gave them all a bloody good laugh when our goalie, Robert Green, let a tame shot slip through his fingers and dribble into the net. How they loved that, the Dutch, the Yanks and anyone else who happened to be in the bar - all except two of course. We held our heads in our hands and wept.

"He must have been on a bung," sighed Rob.

It was the start of another dismal World Cup for us. We scraped through to the last sixteen with a win over Slovenia and then played our old friends the Germans. Everybody raves about how good this young German team were and the score - 4-1 to them - bears this out on paper. What that doesn't tell you is that had Frank Lampard's 25 yard screamer on the stroke of half time not been wrongly disallowed by the referee (it was at least a yard over the line) then the score at the break would have been two all and it could easily have been a very different story. But that's history - and that's the luck of the English!

We stayed in Haarlem for three nights. In between the football we strolled around the Grote Markt where we found the street market in full flow with hundreds of stalls full of cheeses and fruit, cheesecakes and waffles and bought some very nice big juicy strawberries. After a peer into the stunning Gothic interior of the 14th Century cathedral which has somewhat unfaithfully swopped faiths a few times over the years, we sat on the terrace of a small café and added some much needed calories in some stroopwaffles - a sort of sandwich of wafers with caramel inside - with our morning coffee. We strolled around the waterfront and climbed to the platform of the Molen de Adriaan for a fine view over the city rooftops. Suzy went shopping in the Gouden Straatjes district, which translates as 'the streets of gold'. I always thought Dutch was an easy language to understand! Whether this meant that they were paved with gold, or sold gold, or just relieved the shopper of their hard-earned "gelt" wasn't clear, but Suzy managed to find a few bargains. Well that's what she told Mike anyway.

Rob and I took a short rail trip to Hoorn to have a ride on the narrow gauge steam tramway that runs for 20 kilometres to Medemblick. The railway is twinned with our own Bluebell Railway and I think they organise reciprocal visits where members spend a week or so assisting with the running of trains and carrying out routine maintenance work. There are nine steam locomotives on the line, including a former NS (Dutch Railways) 0-6-0 tank engine built in 1914, No 7742 'Bello' and a couple of strange looking enclosed tram engines. Our locomotive for the trip was an 0-4-0 German built tram engine No 26 with four wooden bodied tramway carriages with open platforms at either end. That meant we could stand out in the fresh air and listen to the quiet easy beat of the loco as we trundled north to Medemblick. The journey took an hour and a half, stopping at three or four tiny wayside stations on the way. I made that an average speed of about 12 kilometres per hour - a bit faster than the boat and almost as fast as the Titfield Thunderbolt. At Medemblick there was the option of a trip on the Ijsselmeer to Enkhuisen aboard the steamship "Friesland," but we hadn't the time so returned on the train back to Hoorn where we had a wander around the shed and a chat with the friendly stationschef, before returning to Haarlem on a Dutch Railway double deck regional express.

On our last evening in Haarlem we ate in a small restaurant on the waterfront close to the boat and I had the moules frites while everybody else chose some variety of steak - a decision that I came to regret.

We were heading back to Dordrecht as I wanted to talk to Den Breejen about a few small marks in the deck paint. They had done an excellent job overall but unfortunately someone had stepped on a couple of small areas before the paint had completely gone off. This had left shadowy marks which seemed to be just under the surface and could not be removed. It wasn't much but "the ship and a ha'porth of tar", as they say.

So we left Haarlem and steered south, stopping en route at Lisserbroek for a Suzy lunch and to watch Holland beat Denmark two nil. Surprisingly we managed to get an excellent picture on the TV. I had a Zender satellite dish and digibox which wasn't always very reliable. It was a tricky job to set up the dish in the right direction at 152° to get it to work. The TV was of course inside the boat and the dish would need to be positioned on the roof which meant that you had to have someone inside to shout "that's it" loudly when a picture was found, then by the time you'd stopped moving the dish you would get another shout - "no - gone again." The elevation of the dish was also important, something that varied with your latitude, and all these factors combined to invariably end up with a "sod it - didn't want to watch it anyway." Another factor was that the dish obviously sat on a moving object, so at any slight breath of wind or passing vessel, unless you had tied up very securely, the picture would disappear, usually at the critical point when you were just about to find whodunit, only to reappear again after you'd completely lost the gist!

Bonds Werf - Edam

Approaching Haarlem

We only had a small old-fashioned TV, one step up from a Logie Baird Mk 1 I think it was, but to be honest we rarely used it anyway. By some minor miracle however on this occasion we sat through 90 uninterrupted minutes as the Dutch did what we lived in vain to see England do, destroying the Danes with a masterful display. Two Liverpool players were involved with both goals, Daniel Agger unfortunately deflecting the ball into his own net, and Dirk Kuyt finishing off the Danes five minutes from time. I do think Internationals have lost their edge a bit these days, when you recognise half the players from English teams. The old mystique of World Cups of the past with unknown and sometimes exotic talent from distant and little known parts of the World suddenly coming to fame on our TV screens. In this game alone there were thirteen players from the Premier League - Stekelenburg, Heitinga, Van Bronckhorst, Kuyt, De Jong, Van Persie, Robben, Vorm and Afellay for Holland and Sorensen, Agger, Bendtner and Eriksen for the Danes! It could just as easily have been Stoke City versus Sunderland.

After the game had finished and we were about to cast off, I was suddenly struck with the screaming habdabs and had to make a dash for the heads. I was extremely ill and almost passed out but felt better after about half an hour of serious fretting from all concerned. Even in my darkest moments, I remembered Mike's record as Medical Officer on the Pando Head and there was no way I was going to let him anywhere near me. The first snap of the rubber gloves and I would have been out of there faster than a camel when he hears the swish of two bricks! I had some Gaviscon on board and that did seem to settle the stomach a little.

We continued through the upper shores of the Kaag and into the Brassermermeer once again. I was still feeling too fragile to eat and had been drinking nothing but water all day. We put it down to a dodgy moule, being the only thing we could think of that I'd eaten and no-one else had. I took to my bunk while the rest went ashore to a restaurant in the Sailing Club. The next morning I was still feeling a bit on the delicate side but managed a couple of slices of toast. We retraced our steps to the Kaag and followed a narrow channel on the western edge of the lake which took us back to Warmond where I found a small clinic with an almost over-friendly receptionist and a very unfriendly doctor, who without even examining me, diagnosed a bladder infection and prescribed a course of anti-biotics, which they conveniently had on the shelf. The only time he broke into anything like a smile was when I handed over the fifty Euros for the ten minutes of his time and the 24 little pills. The over-friendly receptionist then gave me a receipt which she said I could use in England to reclaim the fee from the NHS. In the event I don't think I bothered.

The following day I was almost back to normal (as normal as I ever was, which wasn't very normal!) and we carried on south on the Zijl (pronounced phlegm) over the crossing with the Oude Rhin at Leiden, where we were nearly decapitated several years earlier, to our stop for the night at Delft. Another fine windmill-side mooring in the Centre of the town - a sort of smaller Haarlem with a larger Grote Markt and nothing at all, apart from one thing, in common with Stoke on Trent. Two things maybe on reflection, as they both had used water borne transport to distribute their wares.

From here it was just a short run before the revolving crow's nest on the observation deck of the fifty year old 185 metre tall Rotterdam Euromast hove in to view. You can now come back down from the top in 15 seconds at 100 kph on a rope slide for 52 Euros - I think that means that you have to pay, although I don't think I would contemplate it even if they were paying me. After descending the lock at a rather more sedate pace, we turned left on to the mighty Maas once more, dodging through the melee of shipping and passed beneath the iconic Erasmusbrug, which the locals call the Swan, before carefully crossing to the right side of the channel as far out of the way of the heavy tonnage as possible. Vigilance again called for. You never quite knew when you might come under "attack" from left, right, ahead or behind, from some leviathan bearing down on his urgent mission. The currents were quite strong here. I once watched a 1000 tonner doing a U turn to stem the tide in to the harbour at Wilheminahaven, a few kilometres west of here and he must have drifted 3 - 400 yards sideways before finally completing the turn. That's probably not quite true - it was more like 100 yards. I've been told a million times not to exaggerate!

We passed a town on the left with a rather amusing and painful sounding name - Krimpen aan den Ijssel. I think you can get a cream for it in England. I don't know whether it was twinned with Chalfont St Giles but it ought to have been. A bit further on, the site of another potential disaster - Krimpen aan den Lek - plaster of Paris made here perhaps?

We were soon back on our old friend, the Beneden Merwede, and Dordrecht, where we had to make another swift heart-in-mouth crossing of the channel. Judging the closing speed of vessels steaming up towards you can be a bit of a challenge and we gratefully made use of all Mike's years of experience. At Den Breejen we tied alongside the shed once again and went to look for Dijk.

I can't say he was all that enthusiastic about seeing us. He did stroll over, hands in pockets, to look at the problem but just shrugged with a sort of what-do-you-want-me-to-do-about-it sort of shrug. Without completely doing the entire deck all over again he said there was nothing that could be done. I wasn't particularly happy about it but one thing I had learned is that you can't tell a Dutchman how to do anything. They only know two ways - the right way and their way. They were the best - they knew everything and they were perfect - end of story. I did get him to knock a (very) small bit off the bill so there was some small consolation.

As Rob said, "When you shake hands with a Dutchman always be sure to count your fingers afterwards."

We also got a free three week mooring at the yard out of it!

Our train at Medemblick

Chapter 6   La France Encore

The intention for the next leg of our trip was to return via the Meuse and Liege and then the northern branch of the Canal de L'Est back to Toul for the winter. As usual though the best laid plans where boating is concerned do not always turn out as planned and this was no exception.

I took the car to Liege where I met up with Pat and Dobbo who had driven down in the Dobbomobile, and took them back to the boat which was still at Dordrecht. We bade farewell to the Den Breejens and followed the Zuidwillemsvaart to join up with the Meuse at Maasbracht. The last stop on the canal was at the small town of Panheel, about one kilometre from the junction with the Meuse. We set off the following morning and just as we were approaching the turn the heavens opened. It had been getting progressively darker and suddenly the end of the world happened. In a matter of seconds the teeming rain had reduced visibility to less than fifty yards. I could only just make out our own bow just 18 metres away. At the same time I had a nagging feeling that we had turned too soon and were heading into a dead end. The chart wasn't very clear but we had to stop anyway as it was impossible to see anything. After about ten minutes the deluge eased very slightly - enough to start moving slowly again. Pat stood at the prow and shouted that there was another ship approaching. It took several minutes before I saw it - the Marie Celeste - like some ghost ship slipping past. We managed to turn around and tiptoed back towards the turning for the canal. I thought the best thing was to try to get back to our starting point, tie up and wait for things to improve. It was definitely a no-go to try to reach the Meuse with the weather as it was. We picked our way through the curtain of mist and rain, eventually finding somewhere to secure. Everyone was drenched through and the first thing to do was to get into dry clothes and have another cup of coffee. The engine room on Saul Trader gets very hot when we are underway and makes an ideal drying out space. It soon took on the appearance of a Bombay laundry as shirts, trousers, socks, underpants and various other strange bits of underwear that looked a bit like dishcloths, most of which belonged to Dobbo, hung from every available space.

It was an hour before the rain gave way to a flash of sunlight. The warmth soon started to evaporate the water and the decks began to steam gently in the weak sun. I checked the chart again and decided that we had definitely turned too soon. The channel we had assumed was the Meuse was in fact the Oude Maas which was by-passed by the Juliana Kanaal. Now we could actually see where we were going, it did become a bit clearer. At the turn there was a narrow spit of land which we should have gone round and left to starboard. Soon after we entered the canal we were presented with the evidence that we were now in the right place - two very large locks side by side at Maasbracht. There was a large harbour filled with commercials alongside the locks, but it was still only late morning so we decided it was too early to stop. I had been here some years ago by car to visit the impressive works of Linssen Yachts.

Several years before Saul Trader became available, I had considered one of these Rolls Royce of motor yachts. One of them had appeared on the Sharpness Canal. It had been bought by a former boatman, Roy Beckett, who had worked for Harkers in the Bristol Channel and knew a bit about boats. He had bought it in Holland and sailed it back to Bristol and he couldn't speak highly enough about it. That was the one big advantage of course - these boats were built for dual purpose and were equally at home on the canal or at sea. The most common in the range was aptly named the Sturdy and sported an odd looking flat shaped bow and heavy duty rope rubbing strake. There are many Dutch boat builders turning out this type of vessel but Linssen were considered the best - well certainly the most expensive. We were given a most friendly reception and shown around the factory by a very tall Dutchman who went by the name of Willy. He took us through the various workshops where there were probably 30 or so boats in various stages of completion. There was a very efficient production line and the boats were moved from workshop to workshop as the job progressed, a bit like a car assembly line. What struck me most of all was the spotless cleanliness of the place. You could literally have eaten off the floor. I could imagine what Phil Trotter would have to say about that. They must be shite if they don't make a mess building them, or some such similar put-down.

In the event I came to the conclusion that as superbly finished as they were, they were still only 35 - 40 feet long with a cramped fore cabin, saloon cum dining room cum galley all squashed in together, and a not all that big master bedroom aft with a bathroom and shower that a lot of fat Dutchmen probably wouldn't be able to squeeze themselves into. I do like a bit of space to spread out. I had met a retired policeman from Norfolk who had a similar sort of Dutch steel cruiser near Nevers. He bemoaned the fact that he had a wife and a large dog (I think that was the way round) and they lived permanently on the boat and he could never get away from either of them. It made me think and I came to the conclusion that for a quarter of the price of a Linssen there was over three times the amount of space on Saul Trader. I wrote to Willy to thank him for the hospitality and to their credit I was never bothered again by Linssen with any kind of hard-sell tactics. Come to think of it, they probably had me down as a twopenny ha'penny waste of time - tyre-kicker.

The Juliana Canal connects Maasbracht with Maastricht avoiding 36 kilometres of the Meuse, which forms the border with Belgium and Holland. Once through the lock at Maasbracht, which we shared with two 1000 ton commercials and three other pleasure craft, it was plain sailing in the company of many large commercials, through another large lock until the river Meuse was re-joined at Maastricht. We couldn't find anywhere to moor near the city and finished up in a small yacht harbour several miles away. Four kilometres from here the Julianakanaal joins the busy Albert Canal on the final leg of its course from Antwerp to Liege, then after another five kilometres or so we diverted on to what is known as the Basse Meuse - just for the hell of it really, but also for a bit of respite from the procession of large ships heading to and from the port of Liege. This involved descending one lock, the Lixhe Excluse and then traversing a pretty tree lined canal which led in to the river until after another ten kilometres we ascended another lock at the Ile de Moinsin, to regain the Albert Canal proper that led into the heart of Liege, past the imposing statue of the man himself, King Albert, standing with hand on heart beneath the lighthouse that guards the entrance of the canal.

The river through Liege is crossed by some sweeping bridges which are impressively illuminated at night. We passed a long row of high rise apartment blocks on the left bank before the City Hall and the square red brick building that houses the Curtius Museum of decorative arts, through the Pont des Arches with its four statues set into the piers and then on our left the grand façade of the Aquarium Museum, and the Provincial Palace, before passing below the J F Kennedy bridge. On the left bank we approached the Port des Yachts, which looked inviting as it was protected from the surging wash of passing ships by a dividing wall. We motored slowly inside but as the name suggested it was a port for yachts, well - motor cruisers more to the point, but no room for us. The helpful port Capitan did come out of his office and suggested that we try the opposite side of the wall, so back out on to the river we went. There was just about enough space for us between two commercials and in the event it wasn't too uncomfortable. What is more it gave us a wonderful view of the illuminated bridges of J F Kennedy and Pont Albert which were further lit in the evening by a display of fireworks, and was just a short walk to the centre of Liege and the railway station.

Liege - Guillemins is the impressive main station in Liege and had recently been rebuilt to accommodate trains on the high speed routes. It was designed by the Spanish architect Santiago Calatrava, and as you might expect from someone with a name like that, it is quite an extraordinary extravagance. It is constructed of steel, glass and white concrete and features a stunning glass and steel sweeping roof which looks like a huge whale and would not be out of place in a national sports stadium. The reconstruction cost a mind-blowing 312 Million

Euros and provides 5 platforms and 9 tracks allowing access for high speed trains.

Dobbo tottered off to find his car - he had forgotten where he'd left it actually and Pat had to remind him. They packed their meagre belongings into the boot and I took my car to Namur to meet up with the crew for the next stage of the voyage, my step-son and his son Dylan who, since the day he was born, I had called Percy. We spent the next day in Liege. It was a Friday and we had been told about the weekly Saint Pholien flea market that was held in the Outremeuse district, just across the river from our mooring.

I wondered whether we might find Jean-Luc, the Mike Harding look-alike that we had met years before in Landrecies, but there was no sign of him. Not surprising really as there were hundreds of stalls and masses of people. I think most of the dealers were professionals and so the likelihood of finding that dusty old masterpiece for a fiver was pretty remote. I did find some glass candle-holders - five Euros for three - which I snapped up to replace the ones on Saul Trader that were chipped.

We then crossed back over the river via the Pont des Arches to the Place du Marche with its 18th Century red brick Town Hall nicknamed Le Violette for the obvious reason that it did seem to exude a sort of purple hue. We found a café overlooking the square where we indulged in some Liege speciality - Boulets les Liegeoise - not as exotic as it sounds - basically meat balls and chips, with a dollop of mayonnaise naturally. We walked back to the boat via a circular route past the Provincial Palace and the magnificent Cathedral of Saint Paul.

Next day we headed off west towards Namur. The first lock was some 20 kilometres away. We shared the lock with three motor cruisers, secured our lines and were slowly lifted skywards. This being Belgium, papers were called for inspection and rubber-stamping by the éclusier. I dutifully climbed the stairs to the control cabin high above the lock with a commanding view of all it surveyed. Stamp stamp domp domp "sixty five cents thank you" and I turned to leave. Then Mrs Eclusiere came out with the punchline.

"You do know of course that the next écluse is kaput and will be closed for today."

No of course I didn't bloody know that. Why the hell would I have passed through your lock, as lovely as it is, if I'd have known that.

A quick check in the guide showed that the next lock was about as far again but there was very little in between and nowhere that we could stop as far as I could tell. There was only one thing to do and I quickly made the decision to turn round and go back to Liege. I indicated to the éclusiere my intention and she held the gates open while we did a U-turn in the lock approach, closely followed by two of the cruisers, and descended back from whence we came. We were back in Liege by 1 o'clock and this time there was a space just big enough for us inside the Port of Yachts. I reversed Saul Trader into the narrow gap much to consternation and worried fretting from the adjacent owners of the millions of Euros worth of floating steel, without, as they say, touching the sides. There is another interesting statue at the entrance to the port, on top of which there is a diver balanced on his hands at the top of a steel arc. It is a copy of one that stood at the entrance of the Albert Canal designed for the 1939 Water Exhibition.

Next morning I checked with the Capitan who assured me that the offending écluse had been repaired and was now fully functioning, so off we went again. There was a different lock-keeper at the first lock which was a shame because I had really wanted to tell her how much we had enjoyed coming 20 kilometres from Liege and going up and down in her beautiful lock, just to go back 20 kilometres to where we had started! We passed through the naughty lock without incident and after passing the huge complex of the Tihange Nuclear power plant, stopped for a couple of hours on the river at Huy on a nice little wall with conveniently placed bollards, recommended by Mrs Bradshaw herself, opposite the Collegiate Notre-Dame et Saint Domitien. We went for a bit of a stroll after a spot of bread and cheese, across the bridge into this rather charming little town, and took a quick peek into the exquisite interior of the cathedral. It has some stunning stained glass (I do like stained glass) and a huge rose-shaped window, an incredible 9 metres in diameter. After a small beer and a Coke for Percy, we moved on half a kilometre or so to the refuge of a small harbour sheltered from the wash, once again thanks to Mrs Bradshaw, and settled for the night.

In case you haven't been paying attention, or more to the point if you haven't read the first two books, the wife of a one-time bargee, Mrs Bradshaw, had produced a couple of rudimentary type-written and Roneoed (that's how old they were) mooring guides for Continental boaters. I had bought them for a fiver about 12 years ago from the DBA and I think they were ten years out of date even then, but they were surprisingly accurate and helpful. The only thing you did need to make allowances for were the prices. This little overnight haven cost us 8 Euros - a bit more than the 75 cents of which Mrs Bradshaw had been relieved.

The river from here to Namur becomes quite rural with attractive riverside mansions and rocky outcrops and we overtook Robinson Crusoe, single-handed in a small wooden yacht who waved enthusiastically as his little boat, which looked as though it was crammed with his entire worldly possessions, bobbed up and down in our wake. The railway, busy with freight trains, encroaches on the approach to Namur and the Ardennes forests, and we passed below the bridge in the sky that carries the E411/A4 motorway high above the river and then the boatyard Chantier Meuse et Sambre where we had had a not too satisfactory experience some years earlier. They looked very busy, with several commercials tied alongside on the river awaiting work and more up on the cradles that lifted them high up the bank into the boatyard itself. Little did I realise at the time that we would be back there rather sooner than expected.

Just beyond the yard is the last lock before the river divides - the Meuse veering off to the left towards the French border at Givet and the Sambre to the right towards Charleroi. Unusually we were the only boat inside the vast chamber but as the gates started to close behind us, a small blur came puttering around the bend and the lock-keeper stopped the operation, swung the gates open again, and in came a grinning

Robinson Crusoe complete with a beard that made him look as though he was in the process of swallowing a cat.

He must have been in his late seventies at least, and Captain Crusoe told us he was heading for the Mediterranean. I offered him a rope which he gratefully accepted and we ascended the lock tied together. In Namur we turned on to the Meuse while our intrepid adventurer took the Sambre route. We didn't see him again until several years later when he passed us in Chagny heading north on the Canal du Centre. We moored below the Casino for the night, and the following day at the lovely town of Dinant, where Mark and Percy did the obligatory tour of the Citadel while I did the obligatory boat clean-up. We ate on the quay and I went for the moules frites - some people never learn.

The river from Dinant to the French border at Givet is delightful, passing as it does through the forested Ardennes. It is wide and deep with sweeping bends and few locks. It has a wonderful fresh and open feel which was really enjoyable. Vessels of up to 650 tons can reach Givet but after that the French Freycinet gauge locks restrict tonnage to the 38 metre 300 ton peniches.

The Meuse rises in the East of France at Chatelet sur Meuse and flows for 975 kilometres north through France, Belgium and Holland, merging with the Waal and the Beneden Merwede channel that passes through Dordrecht, before reaching the North Sea. From Givet the canalised river Meuse, or Canal de L'Est (Branch Nord), runs south to join the Marne-Rhine Canal near Commercy. That's where we were heading, to turn left for Toul and our winter hivernage. The best laid plans and all that!

At Givet, there was no room on the extensive town quay so we turned around and tied up on a wall north of the town. There was an interesting model shop across the road which unfortunately only opened at weekends. I spent a few minutes with my nose pressed up against the window but there was nothing that particularly tempted me enough to wait for three days until Saturday!

A few kilometres south of Givet via a tight almost hidden turn, a narrow channel leaves the river to the right, leading to a lock, closely followed by the 500 metre long Ham Tunnel. Unlike some of the longer tunnels, this one was not lit. The roof was rough-hewn out of rock and as I found to my cost was not at the same level all the way through. Half way in we heard that horrible scraping noise that was the wheelhouse roof coming into contact with jagged bits of rock. I slowed right down and we got out the searchlight - something in hindsight we should have done before - which helped us steer clear of the protruding obstruction. I found out later that had I asked the lock-keeper, he could have lowered the pound by a few inches while we went through. However, too late for that and in the event no great damage done. The Halte Nautique in an arm off the canal at Revin was full to overflowing, so we had to make do with a mooring upstream of the lock approach, in a pleasant spot against the wall overlooking the freshly fragrant weir.

Mark and Percy were leaving at Charleville Meziers and I had decided to go back to England myself for a few weeks. We arranged a mooring inside the Port Fluvial at Charleville. I usually stow any loose items from the deck in the for'ard locker, including any ropes that are not being used, and in the event it was lucky that I did. I descended the steel ladder with a coil of rope over each shoulder and stepped into a pool of water. Where the hell had that come from?

I quickly threw the ropes back on to the fore deck and started to investigate. I hated having water anywhere inside the boat, and although the for'ard locker had a watertight steel collision bulkhead it was still full of a lot of things that really shouldn't be getting wet, including the two electric bow-thruster motors.

I started frantically chucking some of the untidily stowed items up on to the deck so that I could find out where the water was coming from. It couldn't be rainwater as we had enjoyed a dry spell of at least two weeks. This meant moving the heavy Avon inflatable in its stowage bag and heaving it up on to the foredeck where Mark and Percy dragged it away. There were the dinghy bottom boards, several spare fenders, blocks and tackle, and two heavy turfor winches that had to be moved before I could get to the floor boards. There was an inch or so of water in the bottom but it still wasn't obvious where it was coming from. After shoving more gear up out of the way - deck chairs, rope, canvas and lifebelts, I could see a trace of water coming from the bottom of the starboard bow-thrust motor - the very one that Otto had supposedly sorted out back in Dordrecht. I cursed him and then cursed him again. This was bad news. I couldn't leave the boat for three weeks leaking as it was. The only thing for it was to take off the motor housing and try to temporarily seal the leak. Mark suggested mastic and as it happened I had some left over from a job we had done on the engine room skylights. A few blobs of this around the offending area and the leaking stopped. There is a bilge outlet in the space and I started the engine to activate the pump, opened the valve, and waited, watching for the tell-tale sign of the water going out over the side. Unfortunately this did not happen and I then remembered that it had failed before. I think there must have been a blockage in the pipe as all the other valves operated without a problem. It was one of those jobs I'd put on the "must-do-one-day" list which had been completely forgotten. A classic case of out of sight out of mind. So it was a case of bucket and chuck it. I mopped up with a sponge, Mark hauled the buckets aloft, and Percy chucked the water over the side. What a team! After about half an hour I was satisfied that we had cleared it all. It was early evening - we were all hungry, so I suggested we go eat and take another look at it on our return. We left the hatch cover open to allow the damp to dry out and walked across the river footbridge to the beautiful Place Ducal for seafood salad. The mastic seemed to be doing its job and on our return there was no more evidence of a leak which was something of a comfort. I checked again in the morning but all seemed stable. I told the Capitanerie about it and they agreed to keep an eye on the boat and let me know if there was any change, and with some reluctance we returned to England as planned.

A disciplined ship is a happy ship - Mark, and Percy

Albert at the entrance to his very own canal

Busy lock on the Meuse

Chapter 7   Retracing Steps

Back in England I contacted Vetus in Southampton and although they were very helpful they told me that they did not supply seal kits and the only alternative was a complete bottom end at the cost of an arm and a leg! It really didn't leave me with a lot of choice and the next problem was to find somewhere that we could get the boat out of the water to fit the new part. There was a boatyard at Pont a Bar, 15 kilometres to the south at the junction with the Canal des Ardennes, which after all was in the right direction, but they told me they were busy and wouldn't be able to do anything for at least a couple of months. That was no good to me and after trying another French yard that Gil told me about with the same result, I started to look in the other direction, back in Belgium, and our old "friends" at Chantier Naval Meuse et Sambre.

Christian was not around when I called them, probably away negotiating another deal to build a multi-million Euro cruise ship, and I spoke to his assistant, Phillipe. He told me to get to Namur as soon as I could and call him again and he would see what could be done. There was little choice so I drove back to Charleville with Mike, a Vetus bow-thruster tail-piece, and two new propellers. As we were going to have to pay to be taken out of the water we might as well check both thrusters. There were two on Saul Trader, one each side, as when the boat was built, Darrell thought that the one they had originally fitted was not man enough for the job.

I could usually manage with one, something I quite regularly had to do as one of the protective guards was missing which meant that any bits of twig or plastic could get fouled and cause the sheer pin on the prop to break. Scragg had worked on them a couple of times in the past, which involved him ducking underwater from the dinghy - not a particularly satisfactory, or healthy arrangement. I had asked Otto to replace the props and fit a new guard, neither of which, as it turned out, he had done.

When we got back to Charleville the first thing I did was to check the for'ard bilge which thankfully was still bone-dry. We arrived at Namur two days later on a Friday morning and tied up once again under the Casino at 10.30am. I called the yard and Phillipe said that they were closing for the weekend at 12.00 midday but if I could get there by eleven they would be able to get us out. I didn't tell him that the leak had been sealed and I rather think he was under the impression that we were slowly sinking, but it didn't hurt that he was treating the situation as a bit of an emergency. We motored around to the lock as quickly as we could and got to the yard at five past eleven. Phillipe came down to the quay and told us that they would be ready to haul us out at 11.30. Then the heavens opened with a vengeance. They certainly know how to put on a storm over here. The river steamed and hissed and the visibility was so bad that I could only just discern the guide posts that marked the submerged cradles that we needed to line up on before the lifting could start. Out of the deluge a yard hand came running down the bank towards us waving his arms. He was wearing just a T shirt and shorts and steel toe-capped boots and he was absolutely drenched through but seemingly oblivious to it. He lined us up on the poles and once he was happy we secured the ropes. He then went back to the top of the bank, started the winch engines, checked with his thumbs that we were ready, pulled a lever, and with a gentle jolt we started to move sideways out of the water. Creaking and squeaking we were slowly lifted fifty feet or so into the yard, as the water drained off the boat back into the river. It was five minutes to twelve and our winchman, who it turned out was Polish, disappeared with a wave for his weekend break. I wondered whether he would actually bother to change into some dry clothes before he left.

As soon as the rain stopped, Mike and I got on with the job. We got the old unit out and had the new part fitted by mid afternoon. The new propellers we had bought were five bladed as opposed to the old ones which only had three. The port side prop had completely disappeared which was strange and I wondered whether Otto had actually even bothered to fit one.

107

High and dry on the stocks at Chantier Naval Meuse et Sambre

We fitted the new 5 blader and replaced the starboard one. Otto had made no attempt to fit a guard and unfortunately we could do nothing about that as the studs had broken away from the hull which would mean a welding job. Anyway it was an improvement and we had the job sewn up by tea time and were feeling pretty pleased with ourselves.

On the Sunday I had to go by train to get the car from Charleville. This again proved something of a logistical exercise as it meant going from Belgium into France. As the crow flies Charleville is 140 kilometres - one and a half hours by car, and even as the boat wallows it is only 130 kilometres (and 27 locks). Had I been at all sensible I would have taken the obvious route - train to Dinant, bus Dinant to Givet and then train to Charleville, but God help me if I ever start to get sensible.

I like trains and I'm not overly keen on buses and coupled with the fact that there was only one bus from Dinant every four hours and as far as I could make out didn't always connect with the train, probably combined to help me decide to do the whole journey on the railway. The train service in France is generally very good. In fact it's excellent if you want to travel from say Paris to Lyon, or Marseilles, or from Paris to any of the major cities of France and all of Europe in fact. Where it falls down slightly is when you want to go to or come from Namur to Charleville Meziers. And that is what I needed to do. Namur to Charleville Meziers. By road It's a simple hour and a half trip. By train it is a bit more difficult. For a start it crosses the Franco-Belgian border. Not that you would know it's there these days - no customs, no police, no passport control. Not even a menagerie lion! What it does mean though is that the trains don't go across it - at least not in many places and not via direct routes. Unless, that is, you want to go to Paris.

The first stage was easy enough. Namur to Lille Flandres with a quick change in Tournai. I left at half past two and arrived in Lille two hours later. I checked the departure board and saw that the next train to Charleville did not leave until half past five, which gave me an hour to get a bite to eat before I left. I needed to buy another ticket for this leg so I approached the booking office and spoke to the bespectacled young man behind the glass partition.

"Un simple à Charleville Meziers s'il vous plait."

Well by the look on his face I might have been asking for a single to the moon. I said it again but still not a flicker of recognition. Why the hell is it that these French don't understand their own bloody language?

"Ch - arr - veel Mets ee ay." I wanted to add "it's a town - in France," but refrained for reasons of diplomacy. A girl in the queue behind me was getting impatient. I turned to her hoping that just maybe she'd heard of the place but I drew another blank. Finally I indicated for paper and pen and wrote it down, slipping it under the slot at the young clerk.

He glanced at it quickly, beamed with a beam that looked as though he'd just discovered the meaning of life and said.

"Ah - Charleville Meziers. Why did you not say?"

I managed to get hold of an English newspaper and settled down to spaghetti bolognaise in one of the station cafes. The train was one of those smart new double-decker cigars and I clambered up the stairs and settled down to enjoy the view and the crossword. The journey time to Charleville was just over two hours and by departure time the train was pretty well full with shoppers and workers going home from their days' labours. It was quite a fast train but stopped at several places along the route gradually decanting its passengers. Templeuve, Orchies, Saint Amand les Eaux, Valenciennes with its extensive sidings full of freight wagons awaiting their overnight journeys to all corners of Europe, Le Quesnoy, Aulnoye- Aymeries, and Hirson. All these stations came and went with the minimum of fuss and a single recorded announcement over the train's PA system. There was none of the banal repetition that you get on English trains, that assume we are all thick and ignorant - "We will shortly be arriving at Trumpton your next station stop - mind the gap when leaving the train - please remember to take all your possessions with you - please do not leave luggage unattended - please familiarise yourself with the safety notices - please don't forget to get off when you reach your destination - please do not use your mobile phone in the quiet carriage - please do not get off the train when it's still moving - Trumpton your next station stop - thank you for travelling with Last Little Western - please take care when leaving the train - PLEASE JUST SHUT UP!"

I was on a Virgin Cross Country train a few years ago which was one of those tin cans on wheels with three and a half coaches that they use on the longest possible routes. This one had started at Penzance at o Christ double o and was going to Aberdeen (arriving at o Christ double o plus one day !)

Fortunately I only had to endure it between Banbury and Leamington Spa. I was in the "quiet" coach and sat back to savour the delights of the Warwickshire countryside. Suddenly the peace was shattered by the guard, a Brummie from Dudley with obvious aspirations of becoming an international darts commentator. In case there was anyone on the train trying to get a bit of sleep and might miss the vital information that he was about to impart, he had turned up the volume on the PA to Mach Six.

"Good arfternoun liedees and gentlemen buoys and gurls, and welcum aboard this Virgin Trines o foive twenty foive survies (*that's a joke too isn't it - what service. They should be done under the Trades Description Act*), from Penzance to Aberdine calling at Leamington Spire, Birningum Now Strite, Tamworth, Dorby Midland, Chesterfiled, Wakefiled Westgite, Lieds, York, Dorlington, Durrem, Nowcassel, Alnmouth, Berwick, Edinburrow, Cupar, Lewkers, Dondie, Arbrowth, Montrows, Stonehiven and Aberdine, where we were dow to arroive at twenty thry fifty noine but unfortunately dow to signalling, starffing, mechanical and one our toe other problems we are running approximately fifty noine, foive noine, minutes lite. We apologuise (*lies*) etc etc etc."

Then all was blissfully quiet and peaceful for fully one minute when.

"Good arternoon all. Sid 'ere your buffet car hattendant speakin'. The buffet car his sit-u-ated in Coach D. We 'ave for you today a selection of cold drinks, sandwiches hand rolls, crisps, choclate, pies hand cakes for your consummation. Unfortunately there is no tea or coffee available today as the boiler 'as blown up. Thank you."

I am not making this up. Any poor bastard who happened to be making this marathon of a nineteen hour - no sorry, plus 59 minutes - journey would have to make do without the small comfort of even a hot drink to lighten the misery and go some way to preserve sanity. And another thing - they are not Buffet cars at all because they have no seats. The train operators are much too mean to provide a seating area as they are too concerned with cramming as many people into their three and a half coaches as possible. I had to sit through all this in the "quiet" coach. God knows what it must have been like in a noisy one! By the time this pantomime had finished we were approaching Leamington where I thankfully got off the train, taking all of my possessions with me and taking care to mind the gap between the platform edge and the train!

The last laugh, as it were, was on me on this occasion. When we reached Hirson there were only about half a dozen people in the carriage and they all got off, leaving me alone, the solitary remaining passenger. OK, I mused, so there's no-one else wanting to go to Charville then. The train was stopped for about ten minutes which I thought was odd but eventually it started to move - in the reverse direction. No problem, I figured, we obviously go back from here on to the main line for Charleville. After a couple of hundred yards, however, we came to a juddering halt. Now one of the problems with these modern trains is that you can't open any windows and look out to see what's going on. After another five minutes or so the lights went off and the generators stopped, and it dawned on me that we had shunted into a siding and were going no further. The second problem with modern trains is that you can't just open the bloody doors, so there I was, stranded on a disabled train in a siding about 100 miles from where I was supposed to be going. I won't say I actually panicked, but I was getting slightly worried, thoughts of spending the night imprisoned on a train crossing my mind. I pulled at the door without success and then saw the emergency switch. Well this was an emergency of sorts, so sod it, I pushed the button and low and behold, the doors slid slowly open. As I jumped down on to the ballast, an orange-suited gentleman carrying a bucket and mop came strolling towards me. The grin that he gave me

112

indicated quite clearly that he had found another idiot who had forgotten to get into the front four coaches - the ones that had just left for Charleville, and had been shunted into the siding in the rear four coaches that were going nowhere until six o'clock the next morning..

Quel dommage! Donner und Blitzen and bugger it!

He led me back across the tracks to the station, all the while wasting his time by muttering his condolences in French. The Chef du Gare was very sympathetic. He was very sorry that it was a Sunday and that it was the last train of the day to Charleville and that there were no more trains to anywhere from Hirson so that I couldn't even go back to Aulnoye and maybe catch a connection. He was very sorry that my only alternative was to get a taxi and he was even more sorry that all the taxis had gone home now that there were no more trains to provide them with business. I had begun to think hotel but looking around it seemed pretty unlikely that Hirson would run to any such convenience. But not to worry. The Station Master hadn't got to where he was today by being indecisive and weak in times of crisis. Certainly not! - He had a telephone and he had the number of his friend who would be only too pleased to run me to Charleville for the not unreasonable fee of 100 Euros!

Pas probleme monsieur.

By the time we got back to my car at Charleville it was 10.00pm - the journey from Namur had taken eight hours. I paid up gratefully between gritted teeth and thanked my chauffeur. My car was still where I had left it and still had all four wheels. I climbed in and started the engine and set the SatNav to my destination - Namur. As I slowly manoeuvred out of the port car park, my attention was drawn to a little yellow light on the dashboard. It was the low-fuel warning and a glance down to the fuel computer showed that I had a range of just 45 miles worth of fuel in the tank. The distance to Namur was 138 kilometres - 92 miles. It didn't take a lot to work out that unless I found a filling station that was actually open, I would run out of fuel 47 miles from Namur.

More consternation. In France everything, including filling stations, closes at 8.00pm at the latest, probably earlier on

113

Sundays. I had a sickening feeling in my stomach as I tried to work out a plan. Should I circle Charleville in the vain hope of finding somewhere but risk using up more fuel, or should I press on towards the E411 motorway where there would surely be a 24 hour service area. There were a couple of shorter routes shown but they were through rural areas where I felt sure everything would be securely shuttered. It looked as though the shortest route to the motorway was about 44 miles so it would definitely be a seat of the pants job but I really couldn't see any alternative.

I drove out from Charleville on the A34 towards Sedan using the throttle pedal as though there were raw eggs under my foot. Nevertheless the "distance to empty" reading on the fuel computer seemed to drop by the second. 40 miles, 35, 25 - things were getting serious now and I was starting to get really worried. It was past eleven, a time when all self-respecting Frenchmen were tucked away in bed, shutters firmly closed. Through Sedan where the only sign of life was the smoke from the crematorium and then, a few miles on the other side of the town, an illuminated sign for an Inter Marché supermarket. Oh joy of joys. I even allowed myself to speed up a little and swung onto the forecourt. There were lights on the pumps and I stopped beside the one that was showing gazole. Then my heart sank. These were unmanned pumps and the only way to get anything out of them was with a credit card. I had come across these in the past and I knew that they only worked with cards from French Banks. I did not have a French Bank Account and therefore I did not have a French credit card. I had some cash but what use was that as there was no-one to give it to. The place was surrounded by darkness and silence. It was as though the Third World War had just finished and I was the only human soul left alive. Somewhat bizarrely I started reciting in my head the lines from Bob Dylan's "Talking World War lll Blues",

"I called up the operator of time just to hear a voice of some kind.
On the beat it will be three o'clock,
She said that for over an hour and I hung up."

114

Had that been the case of course I could probably have smashed the pump open but that wasn't a viable option. I tried using my Mastercard in vain hope but it was rejected. I tried a Visa debit card but that produced the same result - rien.

I was walking around in decreasing circles scratching my chin and wondering what the hell I was going to do when I was suddenly bathed in light, and a little red rusty Renault skidded to a halt alongside me. Out jumped a small man with red hair that matched his car sticking out under a baseball cap. So I wasn't the last person alive after all. God had also spared this little hobgoblin. It must be a miracle. It was a miracle all right. My new friend not only had a valid credit card but also agreed, after some hackneyed negotiation in pigeon French and pigeon English, to let me put in 50 litres of gazole in exchange for the equivalent cost in cash.

"Incredible," I said in French, and I think he understood as he shook my hand and disappeared back into the night in a cloud of smoke.

I finally staggered up the ladder at the side of Saul Trader at half past midnight. Mike was asleep on the sofa. As I slumped into the armchair with a cup of coffee, he stirred and opened an eye.

"Good trip?"

He didn't seem in the least surprised that my little jaunt had taken over ten hours.

"Thought you'd probably stopped off for a bit of train spotting," he said sleepily!

Next morning the yard burst into life at 7 o'clock and our Polish friend arrived and banged on the boat to tell us to get ready for launching. I double-checked in my head that all seacocks and valves were closed and with a lurch the cradles started to grind and squeal again and we were on our way back down the track sideways and into the water with a gentle rocking. We waited for half an hour and I checked that there were no leaks from the thrusters and then we moved back through the lock to the wall below the Casino. There didn't seem to be any restrictions on mooring so I felt quite happy to leave Saul Trader here for three weeks or so while we returned home. As usual in these circumstances I placed a sheet with my contact details in a window on either side of the boat. This was mainly for use in an emergency although I had been called a few times in the past by people thinking that the boat was for sale.

On this occasion however I got another call, just a week after we had left. It was from somebody professing to be the Skipper of a large freighter complaining that Saul Trader was moored illegally on a commercial mooring and must be moved immediately. That was going to be difficult as I was at least 24 hours away and it was also a bit worrying as he was threatening to have it moved. I pondered the problem for a while and decided that although there was nothing much I could do about it immediately, I would have to get back to Namur sooner rather than later to sort things out. There wasn't enough time to organise any crew so I drove back a couple of days later on my own.I wasn't sure what to expect. Would the boat have been moved, and if so, to where? Would it have been impounded by the Polis and a writ nailed to the mast? In the event absolutely nothing had changed. Saul Trader was exactly where I had left it and there was no sign of any commercial vessels anywhere near. There were no official-looking notices stuck on the window, no traffic warden types prowling up and down and no writs on the mast. I shrugged and wondered what all the fuss had been about - probably just some vindictive busy-body putting his five eggs in where they weren't required.

I had brought enough food with me from England for four or five days, so after finding somewhere to leave the car, close to the station, I set off, single-handed, for the long voyage to Toul, 342 kilometres and 82 locks away. The first stage to the French border at Givet is relatively easy for the solo boater. I shared the first lock with a 600 tonner and a couple of steel motor cruisers. I had learned from experience not to try to rush things in locks. The commercials took some time to get settled and they were quite used to waiting for others to do the same. Most of these river locks had a relatively low rise and it was a simple task of getting a rope around a forward bollard leading astern, so that I could use the motor in forward gear to hold the stern alongside the wall. I was always happy to see pleasure boats behind me as I knew they would take their time getting themselves organised which gave me plenty of breathing space. It always amused me to watch them trying to sort out bits of string, bunched up like knitting wool, and get themselves secured. This usually entailed the fat wife on the bow, scrabbling around with her expansive arse in the air, faffing about with the tangled mess and the captain, in his "kiss-me-quick" hat, cursing and panicking as his little boat refused point blank to come anywhere near the wall. Invariably the lock-keeper would have to come and rescue them by taking their lines for them. These were usually private boat owners, not hirers, and it always amazed me that they never seemed to learn how to coil and stow their lines or indeed how to throw them. Admittedly they were usually playing with bits of unwieldy string, not the easiest to toss ashore, but you would think they would have developed some sort of routine.

It was mid-September and we were blessed with perfect early Autumnal weather. Being on my own did have advantages. I could talk to myself and sing to my heart's content - mostly out of tune - swear at passing boaters if they happened to do any small thing to annoy me, decide exactly when and where to stop without having a committee meeting, and most importantly, not have anyone to upset or offend. It was marvellous and I sailed along through the lush backdrop of the Ardennes Forest, with a glowing contentment. The one thing I did miss was having anyone there to share the moment and savour the most wonderful weather on this most wonderful river.

I reached Charleville in two days from Namur. After the deep manned lock at Givet, where they check your papers, and this time did check my French licence, which luckily was up to date, the gauge reverts to the Freycinet standard, so the maximum size craft was restricted to the peniches, 38 metres long and 5 metres wide. This meant that Saul Trader with a beam of 4 metres, fitted nicely inside and allowed just enough room, on most occasions at least, to enter locks without touching. This wasn't always the case however. Sometimes, through a lapse in concentration, or an unseen cross-flow wash, the bow would be slowly swung towards one of the gates, and a quick burst of bow-thruster or reverse gear would have to be employed to save the day. Even then there were times when all that failed - either because of too much weigh or of reacting too late, with the result that the boat would go sliding along the gate before bouncing clear. We used composite zig-zag fenders along the length of the boat and these could sometimes catch in the lock mechanism or get caught under the walkway in the gate and fly up in the air before one or both securing lines snapped and they would end up in the cut with a splash - a bit embarrassing when there was an audience of gongoozlers, which was invariably the case. At 50 odd quid a time they weren't something that could be discarded willy-nilly so a bit of fishing with the boathook was required to retrieve them.

I took particular care in the tunnel at Ham and used the searchlight to illuminate the jagged bits of roof which alleviated any more damage to the wheelhouse. At Revin the lock was quite deep and the bollards were set back from the sides so far that they were out of my sight. I knew roughly where they were and threw my bite of rope in the general direction, more in hope than expectation. Expectation won this time and the rope came back to me snaking down the wall. It was now of course sodden and heavy, or sodden' heavy if you like. Some locks have a white line painted a few inches from the top of the lock-side to indicate the position of the bollard, but not this one. I tried again with the same result. I then tried standing on the cabin roof for extra height but still the bloody thing came slithering back. My arms were starting to get tired and I was about to go to Plan B and climb the ladder with the rope to physically place it over the bollard. Sod's Law again meant that the ladder was at least 6 metres behind the boat and I would have to reverse back to get myself on to it. All this was taking up time and patience and at that moment three young lads arrived and peered down at me from the top. I indicated my plight and although at first they seemed reluctant to understand I eventually got the message across and threw them the rope. After much pointing and twirling of hands they realised what I needed, turned the bite around the bollard, and

118

dropped the end back down to me. I quickly secured it to the for'ard bits and we were in business at last.

These locks are automatic. On the approach there is a rod that hangs from an overhead wire which sets off the lock operation with a simple twist. Once inside the lock and secured the filling/emptying is started by lifting a rod set in the chamber wall and when this cycle is complete, the exit gates open with a flashing warning light and a beeper and off you go.

I took a Euro note from my pocket intending to reward my assistants with the money for an ice cream but alas they had vanished, probably afraid that I might give them another job.

From Charleville I had another 215 kilometres and 55 locks to go. I was leaving each day in time for the first lock opening and continuing as long as I could, stopping for half an hour or so for lunch. As I've said before, whereas on the narrowboat you can often take it out of gear and let it drift about in the middle of the cut while you nip below and put the kettle on, then do the same when you hear the whistle and rush back down to pour the coffee. In quiet stretches you can even rustle up a quick sandwich as well. Not so in France with a barge as there is usually a lot more going on and you can hardly leave a 60 ton boat to fend for itself with the likelihood of a 350 ton peniche appearing, so tying up is essential. I do sometimes leave it tied to a lock pontoon with a single line and leave the motor in forward gear, but even then you need to keep an eye out for other boats that may want to use the pontoon. The VNF nowadays has started to get a bit more "official", not I hasten to add, "officious" like the bully boys of the C&RT in England, but notices have been appearing on the pontoons at some locks with the message stating that they are to be used only whilst waiting for the lock. This is all very well, but there are very few alternative places to moor on some French canals and I think, like most things French, there is still a certain amount of laissez-faire, thank goodness - something that the C&RT could well adopt. (*no chance - Ed*). It's also quite nice to be able to shut off the engine and enjoy your baguette and cheese with a bit of peace and quiet.

At Pont a Bar I continued straight on, venturing on to a stretch of the navigation from Sedan to Verdun which was a stretch of new territory for ST.   At Dun sur Meuse I moored with a couple of friends whom I had met in Toul some years earlier, David and Jill on their lovely Tjalk, "Owlpen", named after the village where they lived in the Cotswolds, not far from Stroud and just up the road from Uley, where the amber nectar is brewed. David had lost a bow fender and as I had one spare I gave it to him in return for an evening meal - one of his spaghetti specialities. Two days later I regretted my gesture when one of my fenders punctured in a lock and I had to swop it over with another one which was in a less vulnerable position.

I was managing an average 45 lock/kilometres per day - that's kilometres plus locks (divided by 2) and I was quite happy with my progress, so much so that I gave myself a little reward by stopping to watch the Singapore Grand Prix qualifying at St Mihiel. I paid the price for stopping a bit longer than I needed to as when I came to leave I found the lock had closed for the day. It wasn't a problem as I had been making good time and was now only a couple of days, given a fair wind, from Toul. In fact I was so pleased with myself I stopped early again the next day at Euville to watch the race - so there - and still had time to negotiate the final 4 locks at Troussey before turning left on to the Canal de la Marne au Rhin, and tying on the Halte Nautique pontoon in the quiet village of Pagny sur Meuse.

The race incidentally was won by Fernando Alonso. Hamilton retired after colliding with Webber after a safety car deployment when Bruno Senna and Kobayashi crashed on Lap 31.

The following day I passed through the tunnel at Foug and descended the chain of 12 locks to the harbour at Toul. I had completed the 241 lock/kilometres in 38.5 hours at an average speed of just over 6 kph - not bad going even though I say it myself. I had been preparing for the usual "reception" from Madame Touloise and had put on a full suit of body armour, crash helmet and steel-capped boots, but as it happened this proved totally unnecessary as the Madame had left the post and had been replaced by a large magnanimous gentleman who introduced himself with a rigorous hand shake, as Jeffery. Actually I have forgotten his name and didn't record it anywhere so he'll have to be Jeffery. It suited him anyway - over-the-top bonhomie and gushing with goodwill. I didn't trust him at all! At least he was friendly and tried to be accommodating, and he was a vast improvement on Madame Touloise.

He arranged a tanker of fuel - 1000 litres - to be delivered to the quay the next day and it duly arrived at 10.00am. I have one large shallow tank on Saul Trader which is situated under the engine room floor, with a capacity of 2000 litres. It takes up virtually the entire width of the engine-room but is only just over 14 inches deep. This obviously means that there is a lot of surface area (mathematicians can work out the area - answers on a postcard please) which could have been the main cause of the diesel bug that we had suffered with for several years before installing a day tank. For this reason I liked to leave the tank over the winter as near to full as possible. I had no fuel gauge (or for that matter water gauge) and all readings had to be taken with a dip-stick. No that's not me I'm referring to, but the rod that was screwed into a tube in the top of the tank. I had calculated early on that 1 inch of depth represented about 30 gallons. The stick was showing 5 inches (150 gallons) and I was going to take another 1000 litres (about 220 gallons) which should give me 370 gallons, or about 12.5 inches on the stick. All very technical but it did give me another method of roughly checking that I had got the quantity for which I was being charged.

There was a filler on each side of the wheelhouse and although there was a small balancing pipe between the two sides, I liked to put half the load into each one to even up the distribution. Saul Trader was prone to blowing back at times and I always warned the driver to take it lentement. This one seemed to know better however and half way through the first 500 litres I heard the ominous bubbling and shouted to him to stop but I was just too late. A small surge overflowed the deck and into the cut. Now the French, quite understandably, get a bit touchy when people spill gazole into their canal. Gendarmes and Pompiers are called into action, expensive chemicals are employed, much shaking of heads (and hands) ensues and bollockings and even fines are issued. Luckily I had some

121

chemicals of my own to hand, specifically positioned to deal with such an emergency, and I squirted my Fairy Liquid on to the luminous pool that was growing into a large jelly fish around the boat. Luckily there was no-one else around - Jeffery had not shown so far - and in the words of Basil Fawlty "I think I got away with it." After he had completed the delivery, at a much slower pace, I checked the dip-stick and the gauge on the side of the lorry, and paid up.

After a cup of coffee and some toast I went off to the town for a bit of shopping and a beer. When I returned after a couple of hours my heart missed a beat. There were two Pompier vans, half a dozen Pompiers, two Gendarmes and a Jeffrey, all engaged in frenzied activity around the stern of Saul Trader. They had pipes across the quay, machines whirred and another Pompiers was spraying white stuff into the water, Gendarmes looked stern and Jeffery beside himself with fretting. I thought my time had come. Banished from Toul sine die, or even worse, from the whole of France. The boat impounded until the million Euro cost of the clean-up operation had been paid!

I sidled past them with as much nonchalance as I could muster - not easy in the circumstances, nodded to Jeffery, and disappeared below. I peered around the curtain as they went about their work, expecting the knock on the door at any moment and the handcuffs. Amazingly, and to my great relief, the call never came and after about an hour they packed up all their gear, shook hands all round, kissed each other goodbye, and vanished into the night. There were a couple of Kiwis, Pete and Cath on a wide-beam narrowboat moored next door whom I had got to know from an evening of socialising with a few beers on the stern of their boat. I crept out trying hard not to look too sheepish. Pete was doing something on the stern of his boat.

"Hi Pete," I said in a sort of matter of fact tone, "what was all that about then?"

"Oh the spillage - that was old matey alongside me. He brought a couple of jerry cans of fuel with him for his boat and I think he must have spilled a bit in the cut as he was tipping it in."

I had to restrain myself from leaping around and whooping like a maniac.

"Well - easy done, "I said patronisingly, "should be more careful though."

I "celebrated" with a demi picher of vin rouge and prawn and beef fahitas in the Mexican restaurant by the station - a close call and I made a mental note to be more careful in future.

I fetched the car from Namur, packed up and winterised the boat and set off for blighty once again, leaving Saul Trader under the watchful eye of jolly Jeffrey.

I decided to take the eastern route home from Toul - via Nancy and Metz to ~Luxembourg and the Belgian E40 motorway bypassing Brussels and Ostende to Dunkirk, where I was booked on a 1700 ferry to Dover. I liked this route: it was usually pretty fast and had the added benefit of no tolls. All was going to plan. I had filled up the tank in Luxembourg at the cheaper price of 99 cents per litre, my GPS showed my arrival at the port 90 minutes ahead of the scheduled departure, and my Ipod was on shuffle mode and treating me to a variety of music from Fairport Convention to Canned Heat. The sun was shining, the traffic was light and everything in the garden was lovely - until just after Liege. I was overtaken by the traffic polis in the outside lane in a BMW. As it passed, an officer in the front passenger seat waved his arm to tell me to stop and swerved in front of me into the inside lane. I dutifully followed, wondering what the hell I'd done this time to upset them. I hadn't been over the speed limit, I certainly hadn't been drinking and as far as I knew I was complying with all the t's and c's applicable on European roads. I had a breathalyser kit in the boot, warning triangle in case of breakdown, yellow flak jackets hung over the back of the seats, and a packet of the little black chevron things that you stuck on to your headlamps when driving at night. I followed them for about five miles before they indicated that they were turning off at the next exit, and like a good soldier I slowed down and followed them up to a roundabout. They turned right, then left, then after several junctions right again and finally after another left and right, indicated right and pulled up at the kerb - outside a baker's! The officer in the passenger seat got out and went into the shop as I sat behind them bewildered. What was this - trial by doughnut? I couldn't contain myself any longer and went to speak to the driver, who was still in the car.

"You wanted me to stop, " I said, "what's the problem?"

He looked at me as though he hadn't realised that I was still following them, and then grinned.

"No problem - my officer wave you to get into the inside lane - that is all."

I had lost half an hour at their expense and I'm sure that had a bloody good laugh about it but I was now lost and in danger of missing the ferry. That was a hat-trick. I should be allowed to keep the ball. The French, Dutch and now the Belgian traffic cops had got one over on me. I didn't want to but I couldn't help laughing myself, and as it happened, the rest of the journey went without any more hitches and I managed to check in at Dunkirk with 35 minutes to spare.

Chapter 8   Bimbling Around

When I returned to Toul in April, I tried to be clever. A bit too clever as it turned out. I had decided to take the same route, east from Dunkirk through Belgium and Luxembourg to reach Toul from the Nancy side - the back door entry if you like (no innuendo intended). There were several reasons for this. We were using the Norfolk Line service from Dover to Dunkirk, which was 30 or so kilometres east of Calais. Although this took about half an hour more than the crossing to Calais, it was cheaper and I'd got to quite like it in a strange way. The ferries weren't new by any means. They were designed to carry commercial traffic predominantly and as such were sparsely appointed. The up-side of this was that there were no coach loads of screaming kids and the food, whilst pretty basic, was wholesome and good value.

You could have a full English breakfast for about £3 if you could convince them that you were a lorry driver - not that difficult if you dressed like a bargee. The service had not long been in operation and at times we were the only private car on the ship. On one occasion we had driven into a completely empty car park and at first thought we had missed the boat. Then in the distance we saw the loader in his orange flak jacket in the far corner wind-milling his arms and directing us towards him. As we approached, I wound down the window and he said,

"Good morning sir. Nice to see you. We had been expecting you!"

We went straight up the ramp into the ship, the solitary car on the whole deck. Like all good things, however, this exclusivity came to end as more and more people got wise, and these days the ships have been replaced with purpose built passenger ferries which are as noisy and overcrowded as all the rest.

It wasn't entirely without it's problems though. In the early days I had booked the return trip from Dunkirk for a 1700 crossing and arrived in good time at the port only to find it deserted. After it became obvious that something was not quite right, I enquired at the gate to be told that there was no 1700 ferry on a Saturday, and never had been. I had booked with an agency and had the details confirmed in writing but unless I wanted to wait until the next morning, I would need to find an alternative route home. In the end I drove to Calais and paid 245 Euros to use the tunnel. I did get a refund eventually after a bit of hassle, but it taught me never to use that particular website again. Since then I have always booked directly with the ferry operator.

The route through Belgium was fast and there were no tolls. East from Dunkirk, the A16 motorway leads to the Belgian border where it becomes the E40. Off from Junction 1, the first junction in Belgium towards Adinkerke, Tobacco Road leads to the smugglers duty free haven, where thousands of Brits risk getting their cars impounded at Dover every day, to take back boots full of illicit cigarettes to England. We did stop here to put in a few gallons of diesel, which was also cheaper than the French price. The reason that I only bought a few gallons was that I knew that the price in Luxembourg was at least 20 cents a litre cheaper, and I had cunningly calculated that I would have just enough to reach the Principality, where I could fill up and save myself a fortune! Lubbly jubbly.

Except that my calculations were not completely accurate. We followed the E40 past the outskirts of Nieuwpoort, Oostende and Brussels, or Bruckshells, as the nice lady on my GPS insisted on calling it, before veering off on to the E25 via Liege and into Luxembourg. I was being particularly careful to keep a lookout for the traffic Gestapo and avoid the middle lane whenever I could.

Here might be a good time to mention the words "plans laid mice men and best of ", not necessarily in that order. As my dear old friend the fuel computer continued to show a lower and lower reading, so Luxembourg seemed to get further away. They must have bloody moved it out of spite. What I hadn't reckoned for with my mathematics was that the E25 actually skirts the Principality for three quarters of its length, before sweeping to the left and entering the Country close to its southern border. The result of this, to cut a long story short, *(you are joking - Ed)*, was that with the 'miles to empty' mockingly showing a three, I was still 12 miles from the border. At 20 miles I had 'phoned the top mechanic at my local Land Rover dealer, John Otton and posed the question.

"What happens when the fuel reading gets to nought? Is there any leeway?"

"It will run out," John told me bluntly, "and for Christ sake don't do that because it could end up with some every expensive bent something or others which I can't remember - might have been cam rods."

Well - with a very bland and sad looking '3' on the dashboard staring me in the face, I came to the decision, as unpalatable as it seemed, to admit defeat, and drifted to a stop beside a roadside emergency 'phone.

The first thing the voice at the other end said, before I had even had the chance to introduce myself, was "I have to tell you that the call-out charge is 150 Euros that must be paid as soon as the recovery truck arrives in cash."

Oh well that's clear enough then.

The second thing was a sudden cloudburst that soaked me to the skin before I even had the chance to get my anorak out of the car. I didn't want to sit inside on the hard shoulder as there were Juggernauts flashing past dangerously close in a deluge of spray every few minutes and I decided I would rather be wet through and alive than dry and dead. After half an hour the little tow truck arrived in a blaze of orange lights and pulled in behind. The driver got out and didn't even shake my hand or ask how I was. He just said.

"150 Euros." with not even a please or kiss my arse.

I was hardly in a position to make a fuss so I duly handed over fifteen soggy ten Euro notes which he counted twice before taking a 5 litre can from the truck. He poured this into the tank and then spoke for the second time.

"Follow me."

He was a man of few words, was Heinrich.

Off we went slowly re-joining the carriageway until after about 500 metres, around a bend, his right hand indicator started to flash and he pulled off the motorway - into a bloody filling station! Sodom and Gomorrah - 500 metres and I could have

127

saved myself 150 Euros. OMG or whatever it is they say on Facebook. It really didn't bear thinking about. My brilliant scheme to save fifteen Euros had cost me one hundred and fifty - what a genius!

It was now 13 years since we had left England and my thoughts were turning towards making the trip south to the mythical Canal du Midi. In that time we had visited a good deal of Belgium and Holland, and most of the major waterways of northern and central France. We had covered nearly 13000 kilometres and negotiated almost 3000 locks. It was getting close to the time to venture south at last. Paul on the Leeds and Liverpool short boat, "Nidd", had told me many years ago in Landrecies not to rush to the Midi too soon, as there was plenty to see and thousands of kilometres of interesting canals in the middle of France, and of course there was only one route south, via the notorious River Rhone. Notorious that is, at certain times of the year, when flash flooding could raise the levels alarmingly in a matter of hours. This mainly occurred in the springtime, when the snow and ice in the mountains began to melt with a lot of it draining into the Rhone valley. Rob had mentioned doing the trip with "Pisgah" and we made a tentative plan to go together in the Autumn. Rob's son Jules had lived most of his life in France and was now living with his wife Jess in Montouliers, a few kilometres from the Midi at Argeliers. He knew a lot of people and spoke excellent French. He told us that he would be able to find us moorings on the Midi - something that by reputation was not so easy to do as this had become a very popular waterway, due in part presumably to the publicity it had gained from some of the culinary documentaries filmed on board the hotel boat "Rosa" with the TV chef, Gordon Ramsay.

You know the one. His picture is on the packets of Waitrose sausages with the caption below the smiling chef that reads 'Prick with a Fork.'

We made a plan to rendez-vous with Rob at Chalon sur Saone in September to make the voyage south in tandem. Safety in numbers was always a good thing, especially on rivers like the Rhone, and Jules also agreed to come with us. He had a commercial skipper's licence and had made several passages on the river, so his knowledge and experience would be an invaluable asset.

We still had the whole of the summer ahead of us, and decided to potter south along the attractive Canal de L'Est (Canal de Vosges) to the Saone. Jeffery managed to weedle an additional 68 Euros out of me before we left Toul and I spent several days trying to work out how exactly he had done it. I didn't have too much time to dwell on it however as we had opted to take a different route to Nancy, via the port of Neuves Maison, which meant turning right rather than left on the Moselle after leaving Toul. There is a sort of ring road canal around Nancy which always seemed to confuse me. Basically by turning left the Moselle led to the junction at Frouard on to the Canal de Marne au Rhin which approached Nancy from the North. This was the route we had always used previously so we decided on a change. We turned right and took the Moselle west back towards the southern edge of Toul where we had to negotiate a large uphill lock, in company with a huge 1000 tonner loaded with scrap metal. I wondered whether the skipper was the one who had given me a bit of a mouthful a few years previously when he obviously thought that I had not given him enough room on a bend just north of Frouard on the Moselle. We then followed the river past Neuves-Maison to the Canal de Jonction which lifted the canal through 10 locks to the Canal Marne au Rhin where a left turn would lead into Nancy from the South. We continued on the Moselle which at Richardmenil becomes the Canal de Vosges. Confused? Well so was I but hopefully with a study of the diagram below, all will become clear.

The stretch of canal from here to Epinal brought back memories of Keith and Trevor on the hotel barge, Mercator, when Keith had almost cracked his skull in our wheelhouse leaning across the void that led into the after cabin one evening whilst trying to get his hands on a bottle of Jamiesons! There was no sign of them and I had heard that Keith had left and gone to work as a chef in a bar near St Tropez. I wondered whether he had managed to sort himself out but I had my doubts. The Epinal branch canal was closed while they did some work on the aqueduct so we cycled into the town on the

Bromptons for supplies and stopped off on the way back at the bar in the port for a beer.

We arrived at Fontenoy le Chateau in a deluge which cleared just in time for the short walk to the bar. Here we met up again with Roger the Hat, self-appointed King of Fontenoy, and owner of the bar, who invited us back to his house - well one of his houses! According to Roger he owned half the village and quite honestly I had no reason to doubt him. We sat out on a small terrace high above the town around the warmth of a large cheminee and exchanged anecdotes and jokes. Roger's Dutch wife provided some savoury treats and we provided the wine. Roger said that he hadn't heard anything from Keith for a couple of years and so the planned pie-in-the-sky Donny Mo's Pizza Parlour had never materialised. Shame really - I think it would have gone down rather well in Fontenoy.

Roger, like his counterpart Roger the Nose, Joe Parfitt and Gil, had progressed to the French canals many years earlier after a few years of narrowboating. Roger knew our old friend Ner Ner Nicholas and the conversation turned to talk of some of his exploits. Nick was a product of our wonderful public school education system and as such had inherited a sort of holier-than-thou philosophy. He hadn't acquired the plum in the mouth accent fortunately and retained his Leicestershire brogue, falteringly delivered with his unfortunate st st st stutter. Roger recalled a time back in the 60's when they were drinking in the Lord Nelson at Braunston. The new Road Safety Bill had just been introduced followed shortly afterwards by the advent of the dreaded breathalyser. In the gent's loo he overheard Nick and Trevor Maggs discussing the fact that there were no breathalysers on the canal.

"That's one thing about it," said Trevor, leaning on the wall above the urinal, "you can't be done for being charge in drunk of a boat."

"That's ter ter true enough," Nick agreed, "you can't be done for being ch ch ch charge in drunk of a ber ber boat - not not not yet anyway."

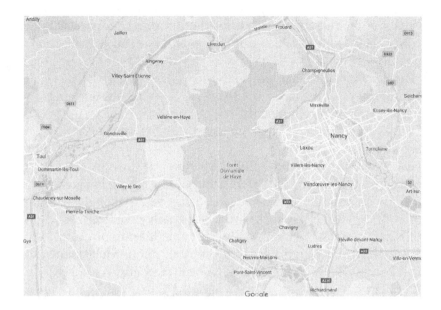

Ring around the Nancy

I recounted a story of the time at the Saul Festival when we were walking on the towpath and a long lost boating friend of Nick's appeared in the opposite direction, accompanied by a young lady whom I knew as his partner in an artist agency business.

"Fer Fer Fairweather," blurted Nick, "Christ you look ill."

Not content with that as a put down, he went on, nodding his head towards the young lady.

"Who's this then, the mer mer missus or the ber ber ber bit on the side?"

How to win friends and influence people!

Nick had a good friend, Miles Tandy, an extremely clever and artistic aficionado of the cut, and every year Miles designed a one-off cartoon Christmas card that usually involved a send-up of Nicholas. They became quite an iconic feature of Christmas, coveted by many, and I certainly kept all mine. Nick seemed to think they'd be worth a small fortune at Sotheby's one day.

The next day saw us at Corre where the Canal des Vosges joins the Petite Saone. We still had a few months to "kill" before the planned passage to the south and so it was a case of bimbling around and revisiting places we had got to know from previous trips. The river here is quite narrow and in some places looks more like a canal. We spent the first night tied on the bank just below the lock at Ray sur Saone and had to utilise the gangplank in order to get ashore for a stroll around the lovely village. There is a wonderful lavoir here with ornate arches that give it the appearance of a small chapel, bedecked with bright red roses and geraniums with a beautiful oval shaped pool. I suppose it has something to do with the fascination of water but I never fail to be attracted to these ancient wash-houses and this one is perfectly preserved, the only thing missing being the women chattering and laughing as they go about scrubbing their smalls. The village is overlooked by a magnificent chateau high on the hill above the village above the Church of St Pancras and the narrow streets of Ray, and we braved the climb to wander around the extensive gardens. There was only one thing for it after that - and beer was duly sought out and procured in a little roadside bar - I think it was Yvette's - where thirsts were quenched and feet revived.

132

This melancholy scene, taken in the early spring of 2002 at Lapworth Lock on the Grand Union Canal, shows barge BIRMINGHAM on its last trip under the captaincy of Steerer Hill. Most narrow boat traffics ceased after the hard winter of 1884/5 and the subsequent Kia-ora Agreement. Due to the high sulphur content of most British coals, steam powered narrow boats such as that depicted here were banned, the future being with co-ownership, time share and Eddie Stoppart.

A couple of examples of Miles' brilliantly satirical Christmas cards

Totally dissatisfied with the lack of breaking wash, Steerer Hill returns one of the prototype training craft to the boatyard for a bigger blade.

Steerer Hill adopts a seasonal disguise to ensure none of his infant crews is caught slacking over the Christmas period.

At Auxonne there was no room on the quay for us so we ventured into the newly opened marina, which was operated by H2O, the people who ran the extensive operation at St Jean de Losne. The marina is on the left bank just above the Pont de France road bridge, and a short walk from the centre of the town. We motored slowly through the narrow entrance and were greeted by a gentleman, presumably the Capitan, who came out of the office, and after asking our length directed us to a linear mooring on the far side of the basin.

"I'll give you half an hour or so to get settled and come over to see you," he told us in perfect English. We duly found our designated spot between two replica British flagged skips - sorry, replica Dutch barges, and squeezed ourselves alongside. Shortly afterwards there was a knock on the door and there stood Le Capitan, receipt book at the ready.

"Hi. I'm Roy," he said holding out his hand, "good to meet you at last."

I returned the handshake, desperately trying to work out what the "at last" was all about, and I must have looked a bit dumb, looking at him open-mouthed. Roy grinned with a knowing sort of grin.

"Not Pedro Roy?" I said hesitantly.

"The very same," said Roy, "sold it last year and bought the Humber Keel over there, the 'Hazelwood.' We're the new harbourmasters."

My first thought was Oh shit, but Roy started to laugh and I nervously joined in.

"Well good to meet you too", I mumbled, "you're mentioned in despatches in my log."

"Oh yes," he replied, "you're in mine too."

We had followed Pedro fully loaded and doing about 0.5 kilometres an hour on an 11 kilometre straight stretch of the Canal de L'Oise à L'Aisne many years ago. I had berated the skipper in French over the VHF , not thinking for a moment that he might be English, and pleaded with him to let us pass, but there was no way he was going to move over. I found out years later from Helen in Paris that the skipper was an ex-pat batelier so my rantings in very bad French were somewhat wasted. We shook hands again and shook our heads, and Roy had the last laugh as he said.

"That'll be 26 Euros then - two nights.

It just goes to show that you never know who you're speaking to.

I once took a delivery from TNT and as I was signing for the receipt I told the driver that I thought I recognised him. It turned out to be Peter Rodrigues, the man who captained Southampton in the famous FA Cup final victory over Manchester United in 1976 and here he was driving a bloody TNT delivery van. What a travesty !

"Bloody hell. Do you think Wayne Rooney will be doing this in twenty years' time?" I said.

There just ain't no justice! After he'd gone I thought I should've asked him for his autograph!

Anyway back in Auxonne. I had found out through the world-wide web that there was a main line steam excursion due to pass through on the following day. It was to be hauled by the magnificent 241 locomotive P17 and was running between Le Creusot and Besançon - something that I could not miss.

I had a rough idea that it would arriving around midday although these timings are always a bit hit and miss to say the least. I had waited by the lineside in the UK on many occasions to watch a steam hauled train flash past only to be thwarted as either a) it had been cancelled, b) it had taken a different route, c) it had failed at Sidcup, or d) most frustratingly, it had passed through ten minutes before I arrived. I once saw some footage of the Flying Scotsman racing through Peterborough when at the crucial moment, a filthy Vermin Voyager had stopped in the platform, obliterating the view. At least in England there was usually someone around who had inside information - the mobile number of the signalman or somebody on the train, from whom you could glean a few snippets, but in France it was a different story. When I arrived at the station I got some encouragement from the fact there were several "hundred" other "gricers" - what's that in French, "surveiller du train" perhaps, or "griceur" maybe, already dotted around the platforms. You could of course tell them a mile off - dirty anoraks, rucksacks bulging with egg sandwiches, ancient 35 millimetre cameras, beer bellies, baseball caps and trainers - and that's just the women! I did manage to get some information from a likely looking lad with spectacles and spots who informed me that the train was "retard quatre-vingts dix minutes." Now even with my O level grade French I knew that meant it was running an hour and a half late. The problem with that was that I didn't know when it was supposed to have arrived and my attempts at finding out the expected time of arrival met with shrugs and upturned palms. At least there was a buffet on the platform serving beer and coffee where I could keep an eye on the platform so that's where I installed myself with an expresso and a pain au chocolat.

Half an hour later the tell-tale signs of imminent orgasm began to surface as the baseball hats lowered behind camera lenses and tripods that had remained static for hours were suddenly shifted up and down, left and right. The train had been sighted - plumes of white smoke appearing over rooftops and the squeak of the whistle heralding the great event. Venturing back on to the platform I made my way to a spot clear of all the budding David Baileys where I could watch the action unobstructed. The first thing that became apparent as the huge machine, gleaming in its British Rail Brunswick green paintwork with red lining came into the station with its headlamps shining brightly ahead and its home depot Le Creusot headboard above the buffer beam, was that it was not tearing through at 120 kph - it was stopping. Camera shutter speeds were quickly adjusted and cameramen rushed around to find more appropriate vantage spots. I always found that watching these so-called enthusiasts dashing around was almost as entertaining as watching the train itself. Most of them were so engrossed behind their viewfinders that they didn't actually see the thing they had come for - the beautiful beast that hissed and spat fire in front of them - and went home to find that their treasured shot had been spoiled by a blurred image of a bald head or the back of a Milletts North Face Gortex rucksack. I sometimes worry when I see overweight grown men who should know better running flat out to reach the end of the platform with their pack swinging from side to side and their tripod dragging along behind. I think for some of them it may have been their last action shot on this earth as over exuberance ended their lives - sacrificed to the great God - steam!

For my part, standing quietly on my own facing the sun - no self-respecting photographer would be seen shooting into the sun - I was surprised to see that this huge and powerful locomotive had been given a rather paltry load of just five coaches. In Britain when we run mainline steam we give them a decent consist - ten or twelve coaches at least and sometimes more. This seemed a bit demeaning for the great beast and I wondered whether they didn't have enough suitable rolling stock (unlikely) or that there wasn't enough demand for seats (unbelievable). These locomotives, the last new design to be built for the SNCF with their "Mountain" wheel arrangement of 4-8-2 (they designate it as 241 in France), had been used in their heyday on long haul heavy express trains of 16 coaches weighing up to 800 tons. It did seem a bit of a come-down. I was also surprised to see that behind the massive 7500 gallon 8 wheeled tender they had coupled a long wheel base coal wagon which had its own crane so that they could replenish the coal in situ without having to resort to the coal lorry in the siding technique favoured in the UK. The other thing I found strange was the puny little whistle which sounded more like an Irish tinker's penny whistle. It was like putting the horn from a moped into a Rolls Royce.

When the train finally departed from Auxonne to continue its journey to Besançon it was with more than a whimper than a bang. None of the thunderous wheel slipping that we used to get with the Bulleid Pacifics, or the rush of excess steam from the pistons or safety valves blowing off at 35 lbs per square inch. No - 241 P17 slid away from the platform with a controlled nonchalance that seemed to say "this load is a bit of a joke - didn't realise I even had any weight behind me." Oh well it was an experience and I did enjoy the sight of this great machine going through the motions and the antics of the desperate photographers with their dreams of that one superb shot appearing on the cover of next month's La Vie du Rail.

As we left the port the following morning, we waved farewell to Roy who was enjoying his breakfast on the deck, no doubt happy that now retired from the carrying life, he no longer had to get his 350 ton cargo on the move before dawn each morning. Downstream from Auxonne the Saone becomes wider and loses some of its charm. Passing St Symphorien and the entrance to the Canal Rhon au Rhin the Petite Saone becomes the Grande Saone capable of passing vessels of 3000 tons to Lyon and the Mediterranean. We slipped into a fine mooring on the quay at St Jean de Losne and sought out our old friend Gilles at L'Amiral, where we politely declined his offer of ommerlette ommerlette for a nice juicy steak and frites.

"We 'ave er le boeuf, we 'ave er le chicken, we 'ave er le porc......."

Over the next few weeks we bimbled (to use the traditional nautical term) around on the Canal du Centre and the Lateral Loire, stopping here and there sometimes at familiar places and at other times at places hitherto unexplored. I took a train from Chagny to collect the car from Toul. This involved a change at Dijon and a 30 minute wait with a coffee and croissant. The basin at Toul is a short walk from the station and as always I approached with some trepidation in the illogical fear that the car would not be where I had left it or that it would be minus a few important parts. Why this worry never left me I don't really know, as I never once had any problem leaving a vehicle for any length of time anywhere in France - or for that matter in Belgium or Holland either. The only times I had experienced any problems were in England - surprise, surprise. I once had a Sierra 4X4 stolen from outside the gates of the marina at Fenny Compton. I had parked the car at half past midnight, and at 8.00 the following morning it had been spirited away, to be recovered two days later in Coventry with £2000 worth of damage. I also had my car broken into outside the Cape of Good Hope one night and my wallet stolen. Mind you I had been stupid enough to leave it on the front passenger seat in full view of the klepto public. I might as well have put a sign on the door saying "please nick me!" Apart from the hassle of having to cancel credit cards and apply for a new passport, the most annoying thing was that I had two tickets to see Christy Moore at The Point in Dublin. I thought the perpetrators might at least have had the decency to leave them behind but no such luck. I did ring The Point but it was somewhat pointless (no pun intended) as I didn't have the seat numbers, An Irishman who did sound very sympathetic told me there was no point (that bloody word again) in coming on the night.

"Well how would I know it was you?" he said, an argument I couldn't really win.

At St Leger sur Dheune we found an interesting brocante shop and bought six very nice crystal wine glasses for ten Euros. *(two of which have since been broken by some clumsy idiot,Ed)*. At Monceau les Mines there was no room to tie in the basin. The knuckle pontoons - the only ones we had any chance of mooring against, were all taken up by small steel motor yachts (probably owned by Dutchmen) that could just as easily have used the inner pontoons, and nobody seemed to be inclined to move despite my appeals. My mood was not much lightened by a female bridge-keeper who kept us waiting for no apparent reason, other than to check that her make-up was all in place by gazing at herself in a mirror for twenty minutes.

We found a quiet bank-side mooring near the small village of Pailgnes and managed to set up the aerial to watch the European Grand Prix from Valencia. The canal runs alongside a rural tree-lined road, the D974 for several miles here and just before the end of the race we heard a powerful motorcycle roar past flat out, engine screaming. There were lots of these escapees that tore through the countryside in France, particularly on Sunday afternoons, and it was really no surprise when we heard the ominous notes of the Pompiers sirens half an hour later. We cast off and as we got nearer to the blue flashing lights an awesome quiet pervaded the scene. Pompiers stood around helplessly in the shock that comes from experiencing death. I don't like to dwell on these scenes. I'm definitely not a rubber-necker, but it was impossible not to see the mangled wreckage of a motorcycle embedded in a tree. Trees are unforgiving and this one had taken a life that only minutes before had enjoyed the exhilaration of the freedom of flight on a motorcycle. A fragile cord indeed. We were very quiet for some time afterwards and it made me think that getting wound up over a tardy bridge-keeper was a bit futile in the grand scheme of things.

We stopped overnight at Gannay and the next day had another little contretemps with a Princess as I forgot my previous deliberations about the "grand scheme of things." Well it was the idiot steering the Princess to be exact. I always let quicker boats overtake me whenever I can but this guy kept edging up behind and putting his nose up my backside in places where it was impossible to see ahead and much too narrow to pass. The result of all this was that I became more determined not to let him get by in direct proportion to him being more determined to get by! Result - bad tempers and frustration in equal measure. Eventually he lost it completely, opened his throttle wide, and forged past on a totally blind bend. His wash caused me to lose control and Saul Trader veered off alarmingly into the bank, as another speeding motor boat came round from the opposite direction. This in turn made our adversary swerve across my bow and plough into the side himself and it was pure chance that we didn't collide as neither of us had any control over our vessels. Curses and shouts from me and the one coming the other way, shakes of fists, clouds of smoke and other nautical terms that should not be mentioned before the watershed. Princess bounced most unladylike off the bank and ran backwards into the oncoming boat broadside. We now had three boats trying to get on to the towpath! I put Saul Trader into neutral gear and dropped the throttle to wait until they had sorted themselves out. In fact I went below in disgust to avoid really telling then their life histories and made a cup of tea.

My old friend Kevin Day, folk-singer, raconteur and piss artist extraordinaire, used to sing a song called The Hire Boatee.

He would introduce it by saying.

"I was on my boat the other day and there was a boat in front of me (this needs to be read slowly in a broad Midlands accent) and first 'ee was goooin too fast and then 'ee was goooin too slough and it was all because 'ee was ...... An 'ire boatee -

140

"I'm a hire boatee I'm a hire boatee
I'm a hire boatee and I am free
I'm a hire boatee I'm a hire boatee
And I've gotta be back by next Monday."

"I passed a boat the other day
I covered it over with my spray
Hahaha heeheehee
Hahaha I spilled their tea.

Gotta do the ring, gotta do the ring
Gotta do the ring 'cos that's the thing
Gotta do the ring, gotta do the ring
Only one week to do it in"

Kevin once bought a little boat that had sunk in the BCN for one penny. It was called Curlew and Kev spent a lot of time working on it to get it habitable and seaworthy until he had almost doubled the price he'd paid for it. It was a small wooden cruiser and was not quite as wide as Kev was long and the bed was laid out across the boat. Kev got over this small problem by cutting two holes in the side for his feet to stick through which was OK as he and his wife Jackie only boated in the summer in those days.

Another modification Kev made to Curlew was in the engine room. Well not exactly "in" the engine room as Curlew didn't actually have an engine room. This was what Kev set out to correct when he bought a second-hand Isuzu engine and a redundant water tank. He ingeniously set up the engine in the water tank, drilled four holes in the aft of Curlew, and hammered four nails in the front of the water tank. Still keeping up? Kev then drove the water tank flat out at Curlew and as the nails went through the holes, Jackie, poised with a mallet, bent the nails over thus attaching an engine room to the stern of Curlew.

Kev was very proud of his achievement and was keen to show off the fruits of his labours.

During the first demonstration he came past at full bore then threw the engine astern, at which point the nails straightened

141

out, the water tank came to an abrupt stop, but Curlew sailed on into the distance, with Jackie waving from the stern and shouting to Kev that if he didn't get something sorted out soon his dinner was going into the cut and he,d be looking for a new wife.

"Agh - won'urt," laughed Kev.

One evening outside the Cape I was invited to dinner on Curlew. My foot stepping on to the gunwhale coincided exactly with a panicky shout from Kev - "Don't step on the gunwhale."

Too late, only by a split second, but enough to rock Curlew to such an extent that the chilli that was simmering away on the stove, slid off and landed upside down on the carpet.

"Agh - won'urt," said Kev as he scooped it back into the saucepan. "few dog's hairs won't kill yer," followed by one of his trademark guffaws that involved a sucking intake of breath and a sort of "eeeek eeeek eeeeek."

Kev's opening salutation was usually "It's a fine summer's morning," and he would utter this if you met him at any time of the day or night on any day of the year. He and Jackie spent many Christmasses on their boat at Tixall Wide near the junction of the Trent & Mersey with the Staffs & Worcs Canal at Great Heywood. Kev would make a point of parading up and down the towpath in the early hours of Christmas morning, regaling anyone who happened to be within earshot with his cheerful message

"It's a fine summer's morning, eeeek, eeeek,eeeeek!"

Not everyone was amused by this however and there were occasions when his seasonal greeting was countered from the depths of a steamed-up narrowboat with a muffled shout of

"piss off back to bed you silly old twat," and other somewhat uncharitable remarks, which quite upset old Kev. I know it's an old well-worn cliché, but they really did break the mould after Kevin Day.

Kevin should have been famous. It is a sad indictment that the likes of Barry Manilow and Rolf Harris became famous (or even infamous) but Kevin Day did not. There just ain't no justice!

I once saw him performing in front of thousands (well 17 and a dog to be honest) in the magnificent auditorium of the

Lichfield Motor Boat and Cruising Club when his teeth fell out in the middle of a very poignant song about some boatman who went up the Ashby Canal and was never seen again. The dentures dropped into the beer of a lady sitting in the front row and as he bent over to retrieve them his spectacles followed. But did this deter him? Did this interrupt the telling of this sad tale? Not at all. With the true professionalism of the troubadour, Kevin carried on regardless to the end of the song with its tragic message.

"Some talk of deep holes in the Coventry's bed
And some say he went up the Ashby instead
There are stories and theories but for all that they say
Neither boat nor the boatmen has been seen to this day"

As Kevin was want to say when anyone suggested that it might be an idea to tune his guitar.
"Agh - it won'urt."
And it certainly didn't!
Back to the subject of boaters going too fast, it's not always the hirers that are to blame. I think it is usually down to those that only boat for a week or so at a time. They dash up the motorway to their boat and for the first day or two are still in the 70 mph speed limit mind set. It takes a while to slow down to the pace of the cut. I have watched the real professionals on both sides of the Channel and one thing that does become clear is that they never rush to get alongside or to get in and out of locks. It is always best to move at a speed where you are in control, and can stop and reverse without the boat veering wildly around. The exceptions are the skippers of the fast short hop ferries that ply the rivers in all the major cities these days. They have big powerful engines, bow and stern thrusters and props that can turn through 180° and can stop on a sixpence. They also have skilled crew that can lasso a bollard at 100 metres and use the force of tides and currents to good effect - and they are stopping and starting hundreds of times every day.
The fast waterbuses that zoom up and down the Chao Phraya river in Bangkok are a joy to behold, their manouvres in and

out of the stops controlled by whistle signals from the crewman.

I have seen narrowboaters coming into a mooring nearly flat out, hitting the bank and then yelling at the wife to get ashore to pull on the rope in a vain attempt to stop the boat. Excuse me but you do have an engine and you do have a reverse gear. Why don't you use that instead of the hapless wife, sliding long the grass like a water skier, to stop your bloody boat. Try explaining to them where they're going wrong and you're likely to get a mouthful of abuse.

Dave and Becks came for a week and we went up as far as Decize where we ate in the Vietnamese restaurant once again and got drenched on the walk back to the mooring in the Le Boat basin. On the way back south we stopped at Genelard where I got another hammering at babe-foot by the Salisbury Singles Cribbage Champion 2007, Dave Baker, retired Postmaster-General, Winterbourne Gunner sub Post Office!

Chapter 9   South Bound Again

We left Saul Trader in the convenient little basin at Chagny for a couple of months before setting out south to the Med, and on the ferry crossing to Portsmouth I managed to slam my finger in a very heavy water-tight door which caused it to go a deep shade of purple and eventually part company with the nail.

In the September I returned to France with Mike and Suzy minus one nail. We had a tanker delivery of 1000 litres of derv at 1.36 per litre and I did a run through of checks to the filters, stern gear, prop shaft greasers and topped up the oil in the bow thrusters and steering gear. We were all set for the final leg to the South, via the River Saone to Lyon and the mighty Rhone. To be honest we rather scooted through this trip. We had chosen to do it in the autumn when the river would normally be at its most benign and less prone to any sudden flash flooding. The goal was to get to the Midi with the minimum of delay and so we had little time to enjoy the luxury of visiting the towns en route. We rendezvoused with Rob and Julian at Chalons sur Saone where we tied on the outside of Pisgah, moored on the high wall of the Quai de la Poterne. There was no ladder immediately available and so Jules Jury-rigged one which sat somewhat precariously on Pisgah's hatch and we all clambered gingerly to the quay high above. It was worth the effort however. Chalons is a wonderful town and I can't understand why the powers-that-be have not seen fit to provide more floating pontoons on the right bank which I am sure would encourage more boats to visit. There is a marina behind the island on the opposite side but as I found out some years earlier, they don't consider anything longer than 15 metres to be a boat! Further downstream there are several more quays but they always seem to be occupied by massive hotel boats or live-aboard commercials. We found a friendly café in the shadow of the Cathedral Ste Vincent where we enjoyed some scallops and a trio that played some good old

Sunset on the mooring at Seurre, River Saone

1960's music - quite appropriate for us ageing hippies. That's another thing we had led the world with- the music of the Beatles and the Kinks, Rod Stewart and the Stones - music that has endured through the decades. France had nothing in comparison, and was probably another reason why so many French spoke good English. We were careful not to over-imbibe, wary of the need to safely re-negotiate the ladder to get back aboard, and of having clear heads the next morning for the start of our trip on the big rivers.

There are just three locks between Chalons and Lyon and then another twelve before the junction with the Petit Rhone that passes the entrance to the canal to Beaucaire before continuing westward to Aigues-Mortes and Sete and the Etang de Thau, and finally to the Canal du Midi. The river locks are between 180 - 190 metres long and 12 metres wide and as we discovered when entering the first one between Gigny sur Saone and Tournous, life jackets are compulsory. Luckily we had enough on board to go round, but it was obvious that until we showed the evidence that we were all conforming, the éclusier, high above us in his ivory tower, was not going to start the lock operation. Quite what you would do if you didn't have enough for all your crew I'm not sure. I think this rule had been introduced after a fatal accident a few years before when two people fell overboard and were drowned in a Rhône lock.

At Macon we stumbled upon another bar with live music and sat outside in the evening warmth, this time beneath the haughty façade of the Church of Saint Pierre, with pork filet mignon and a glass or two of vin rosé. Over the next few days our progress was governed more by sporting events than anything else. At Fontaines sur Saone we found a wonderful vacant sheltered pontoon mooring just downstream of the bridge and opposite the parish church of St Roch en Val de Saone. Saul Trader moored alongside Pisgah and Jules set up Rob's enormous 120 cm satellite dish and we enjoyed a leisurely lunch on board and watched England beat the Argies 13-9 in the Rugby World Cup. England narrowly avoided defeat after Jonny Wilkinson had uncharacteristically missed five penalty kicks and were saved 13 minutes from time by a try from Ben Young - a somewhat unconvincing display.

The approach to Lyon from the North is quite spectacular, dominated at first by the grand edifice of the Basilique Notre Dame de Fourvieres, rising like a fortress on the top of Fourvieres Hill and visible from all parts of the City. incongruously overshadowed by towering modern concrete apartment blocks. We tied up on the Quai Tilsitt just downstream from the Bonaparte Bridge, opposite the Church of Saint Georges, while Mike and Sue went off to buy our lunch from the market. It seemed a travesty that we weren't to stay longer in this beautiful city, but we were on a mission - "gotta get'em on as N - Nick would say- and I promised to spend more time here, and in some of the other fine riverside towns, on the return trip. That, of course, was assuming that we ever did return!

After lunch we pushed on towards the confluence with the Rhône, passing the port de plaisance and the huge commercial Port Edouard-Herriot, out of bounds to the likes of us, and with good reason. The port handles over a million tons of barge traffic each year. At the entrance there is a large turning area where tug convoys of 4400 tonnes can appear without warning. These convoys help to keep lorries off the roads, a single convoy replacing 220 truck journeys. Judging by the amount of trucks clogging the French roads, it seems they still have a long way to go.

Soon afterwards we passed a couple of large shipyards and what is probably the most weird and wonderful architectural (please fill in your own description here as words fail me) cube! The building is painted in bright orange which is supposed to represent red oxide as used in shipyards. It is imaginatively called "The Orange Cube" and to my way of thinking it's just another massacre of a once thriving industrial heritage faked up to convey something supposedly modern or futuristic. Personally I don't think it works. I have reproduced an excerpt of a description by the designer which may make more sense to you than it does to me.

The ambition of the urban planning project for the old harbour zone, developed by VNF (Voies Naviguables de France) in partnership with Caisse des Dépôts and Sem Lyon Confluence, was to reinvest the docks of Lyon on the river side and its industrial patrimony, bringing together architecture and a cultural and commercial program. These docks, initially made of warehouses (la Sucrière, les Douanes, les Salins, la Capitainerie), cranes, functional elements bound to the river and its flow, mutate into a territory of experimentation in order to create a new landscape that is articulated towards the river and the surrounding hills."

"Ah - so that's OK then.

Macon - mooring

and departure

A few years later another contestant in the "World's Most Stupid Designs" competition appeared in the shape of the six storey Euronews building, This is another cube and this time painted in fluorescent green and called - you may have guessed - "The Green Cube." Call me old-fashioned if you like but I really don't like the way these old wharves and dockside warehouses have been demolished to make way to such follies. At least in places like Gloucester Docks the outer shells of the warehouses have been preserved.

We passed beneath the bridge that carries the A6 Autoroute over the Saone and then joined the Rhône at last, passing the Port of Lyon with its huge container gantry cranes on our left and the Lyon Aquarium on the right. The Rhône is a serious waterway, subject at times to rapid increases in height and current. Unsurprisingly there are strict rules that govern navigation. The buoyed channel varies in width from 60 to 80 metres and all the bridges have designated rights of way for traffic in each direction. Crews must wear life-jackets in locks and pleasure craft are bound to give priority to commercial vessels at all times, sometimes being asked to wait for arriving commercial ships for up to 45 minutes. All locks have radio communication and their respective VHF channels are published in the guides. It is advisable to call lock-keepers in advance with details of your vessel's name, your position at the nearest PK, (kilometre post). These are clearly marked on both sides of the river. You must state whether you are a pleasure craft or a commercial, your size, direction of travel, and precise time of arrival. Locks are attributed VHF Channels 19, 20 or 22 and it also a good idea to monitor Channel 10 when on the move, as this is the communication channel for all ships, and is useful to ascertain the presence of other nearby vessels. It is forbidden to pass through locks with ships carrying hazardous cargoes, identified by an inverted cone. These locks are all provided with bollards flottant and boats must be secured to these fore and aft. A red flag is positioned on the dockside when a particular floater is out of order. It is also advised that crews keep an eye on these during ascent and descent and be prepared to cut ropes if they become jammed. It is forbidden to tie up alongside another boat and to enter or leave a lock before all gates are fully open and the green light is shown. You are not allowed to get off the boat in a lock except in an emergency. You are also forbidden to use the engine to manoeuvre during transit. Vast tonnages are carried between Lyon and Marseilles - push-tug convoys of over 4000 tons can be encountered and commercials travel at very fast speeds, pushing mini tidal waves of wash, so a lot of concentration is needed and a sharp lookout maintained, both ahead and behind. The largest ships, especially when travelling empty, have a blind spot as much as 350 metres ahead, so you need to keep well out of their way well in advance. On bends these vessels may need the whole width of the channel to turn.

While all of this sounds at first to be a little foreboding, in practice it is usually fairly relaxed.

Although the chambers are truly enormous and can look frightening, the movement while the locks are filling and emptying is fairly gentle. Also with a channel 60 or so metres wide there is usually a fair bit of room to manoeuvre.

Shortly after joining the Rhône we encountered our first lock at Pierre Bénite, with a fall of nine metres. La Compagnie Nationale du Rhône was founded in 1933 and set up to safeguard the river and its environs and more importantly to oversee the installation of hydro-electric power stations that use the strong current flows to generate their electricity. There are now 33 of these and together they produce 16 billion KW/h annually, some 4% of the national production. And we're still arguing about putting a barrage across the Severn! Having successfully negotiated the lock, tying to the floating bollards and gently descending, we pushed on South.

After passing two more enormous deep locks, suitably attired in our lifejackets, we tied up in a conveniently sheltered Port de Plaisance at Les Roches de Condrieu. The moorings here were situated in a small harbour that had been created when a notorious bend in the river was straightened out leaving a dead arm on the original course. Jules deftly set to work on positioning the dish in preparation for watching another sporting event. Once adjusted with delicate twists from side to side accompanied by shouts of "got it - gone - got it now - gone again - that's it - OK" from the inside the boat we settled down to watch the recorded highlights of the Monza Grand Prix which was won by "love-him-or- hate-him" Sebastien Vettel, giving him an unassailable points lead of 112. The thing that irritated more than anything about Vettel was the way he whooped and hollered into the radio whenever he won a race - quite nauseating.

Rob rigged up the ship's barbecue on the stern of Pisgah and after a bit of huffing and puffing, managed a goodly heat. Watching him in action reminded me of a saying of my Grandmother when she would admonish me for cursing with the seemingly innocuous expression - "blow it" - which was about the only four letter expletive I knew in those days. My Gran was a devoted Christian and even the word "blimey" was taboo in her presence.

"Don't blow it - fan it with yer 'at, "she would tell me.

We feasted on steak and prawns with salad prepared by Sue and roasted potatoes washed down with a few bottles of Rosé accompanied by some tunes on the Ipod.

Next day we covered 93 kilometres and passed through three massive locks in the company of a small yacht crewed by some young jolly sailors on their way to the Med. Some of these locks had a fall of over 70 feet but they were all equipped with floating bollards that were set into the lock wall and went up and down with the rise and fall of the water level. These were very convenient and safe to use and meant that once you had your ropes secured you could retire to the kettle. Well not quite as easy as that as it was always advisable for someone to keep an eye on them to make sure that the lines did not snag around any protrusions.

We swept along past the giant nuclear power station at St Maurice whose two reactors produce an incredible 18 billion kw, ten times the annual consumption of the city of Lyon! Towns and villages came and went - Champagne, which was once the site of one of the several pendulum ferries that crossed the river. These unpowered vessels ingeniously used the power of the current to swing them from one bank to the other on a length of chain, the ferryman pointing the bow away from the side so that the boat was pushed by the current. Downstream movement checked by the cable ensured that that craft was swept in a semi-circular arc until it reached the opposite bank. The one at Champagne was 14 metres long and could carry up to 60 passengers and 15 horses.

One of the towers from which the cable was suspended is still visible on the right bank.

We passed Saint Vallier, where in the early 16th Century, Diane Poitiers, the mistress of King Henri ll, had been instrumental in influencing the King in the cruel suppression of the Protestants. At PK 89 we followed Pisgah to the right past a rocky outcrop known as le Table du Roi, the King's Table, which was marked by a tall post with red and white vertical stripes, and guided boats past an area of submerged rocks to the left. One legend that gave rise to the name was that in 1248 Louis iX stopped here for lunch on his way to free Palestine from the Sultan of Egypt. He declared the rocks to be as "flat as a table" and ordered his aids to bring food and wine from the locality.

Peter and Paul kicking up a spray

We were blessed with some fine autumnal weather - bright sunshine and a fresh breeze from the south that caused a gentle chop. At one point we passed a heavily loaded commercial, its cargo of sand piled high in the holds and with about 18 inches of freeboard. The "Pierre et Paul" was kicking up a mountain of bow wave and passed so close that it sent a cloud of flying spray towards us flecking our faces with a fine cooling rain.

On past Tain l"Hermitage, where the large dolphins were reserved for the huge 100 metre hotel cruisers and Tournon on the opposite bank (maximum length for visiting boats 15 metres!), Valence with its welcoming Port de Plaisance de L'Éperviere and still we forged on regardless, finally following Pisgah into a small creek on the right with a short pontoon alongside a grassy tree-lined wood. This was a quiet sheltered mooring that Jules knew about but unfortunately proved a no-go when the landowner appeared and refused permission. I didn't find out exactly what the problem was but even with Jules and his perfect French and even more perfect powers of persuasion he could not be moved. After a few kilometres we passed through the lock at Beauchastel with a relatively modest fall of 12 metres. It was almost 7.00 and the lock-keeper gave his permission to moor for the night on the pontoon below the lock, and so it was out with the barbecue once again.

It was great to have Rob and Mike with us. It's reassuring to have another boat as a safety precaution especially on big busy rivers like the Rhone. We were in radio contact and kept reasonably close together. It was also a great boon to have Jules along. He was a qualified passenger ship pilot and had a good knowledge of the river and could converse with other vessels and lock-keepers to warn of our approach, which meant that we always knew in advance whether we would be let straight in or would have to wait for the passage of upstream vessels.

The approach into Lyon

Aprés-vous

We made an early start next morning and made good progress on another fine breezy day. We passed the medieval village of Cruas and its somewhat more modern addition, a nuclear power station. Montelimar got me singing the words (well the few I remembered), of a song called Savoy Truffle by the Beatles on the White Album that mentioned the name -
"Cream tangerine Montelimar....." I think it refers to the locally produced nougat.

After another long run of 80 kilometres and three more locks, this time accompanied by a massive commercial, the "Eridan", that filled the lock with inches to spare between the walls, we found a delightful pontoon mooring on the outside of a small Halte Nautique at Port de L'Ardroise. Once again we tied on the outside of Pisgah which gave us an uninterrupted view across the river of a glorious sunset. We were close enough to the town to be able to walk to a bar - first one for several days, and passed a sign indicating another place that we knew by association - association, not so much for the excellent red wine, but for Del Boy Trotter - Chateau Neuf du Pape. I wanted to add "Rodney" but I didn't have an aerosol handy luckily. Call us plebs if you like! No way Pedro!

After the luxury of a bit of a lazy breakfast outside on the deck the next morning, we made the relatively short run to Avignon, a beautiful town on the left bank made immortal by the children's chanson "Sur le Pont d'Avignon," a 15th Century song about dancing on the Saint Benezet bridge. Although it refers to boys and girls dancing "on" - (sur) le Pont, in fact it was so narrow that this would have been impossible and it is thought that the dancing took place "under" (sous) le Pont. It originally had 22 arches but over the years through siege and inundation from the river, many were destroyed and today there is just a truncated section with four arches and a bell tower remaining. As we approached the bridge a large hotel ship, the somewhat ominously named "Mistral" started to edge away from the quay and Jules radioed to ask the captain what he wanted us to do. As a result we held back until he had completed a 180° turn and passed us with a grateful wave.

Avignon is a charming town - difficult to imagine that it had once been described by the poet Petrarch in the 14th Century as "the most foul and stinking city on Earth." He obviously hadn't been to Delhi.

We were secured alongside just beyond the bridge at 1.00pm and spent the afternoon wandering around the narrow streets within the rampart walls and taking in the sights. We watched the street entertainers in the square in front of the Palais du Pape, gazed up at the gilded statue of the Virgin atop the Cathedral Notre Dame-des-Doms (doesn't look a bit like Richard Branson said Mike), and watched the world go by with a beer in the Place d'Horloge. Jule's wife, Jess, joined us for a few days with their lovely black Labrador "Gazole"!

In the evening we met up with some friends of Rob's, Jim and Florence, who took us to the Bar a Manger where we sat outside in the evening warmth in La Place Cloître Sainte Pierre and enjoyed a delicious meal. There are literally hundreds of restaurants in Avignon and it was good to have the benefit of some local knowledge.

Tranquility in the old town at Avignon

Once again it would have been nice to have had more time in Avignon but it was not to be - not this time anyway.

A new TGV high speed railway connection was opened in 2001. The line connects Paris with Marseilles and Nice and a dedicated station was built a few kilometres from the centre of Avignon. Leaving the port and heading south, we passed below the new bridge just as an 18 coach double-deck TGV swished overhead and was gone in the blink of an eye. One day we may have the same sight on the southern Oxford Canal - God forbid! There is naturally a lot of objection to this development in the UK and placards proclaiming "NO HS2" have sprung up all along the route. I have mixed feelings about it. I applaud the expansion and modernisation of our railway system, but I do think this extremely expensive project, (£53 billion and counting) which will cut a piddling 20 minutes from the journey time from London to Manchester, is a waste of valuable funding which could be far better spent improving and upgrading the existing railway, maybe even reinstating some of the "withered arms" that dear Dr Beeching severed in his infinite wisdom. In France the distances are far greater, there is much more available space, and the TGV network has been gradually expanded over 35 years. The LGV (Lignes de Grande Vitesse) connecting Paris with the Channel Tunnel, was opened in 1993 enabling trains to run at 190 mph and cover the distance - 330 kilometres) in under an hour and a half. For 14 years these so-called high speed trains had to slow to a maximum 80 mph (often a lot less than that due to overcrowded paths) on exiting the Channel Tunnel and entering Kent. Great Britain, inventor of the railway and responsible for taking rail travel to the World, was left looking like a dejected and undernourished underdog and a laughing stock. It was not until 2007 that the new high speed link - HS1 - was finally opened after more opposition from the NIMBY brigade, to terminate in the magnificently rebuilt St Pancras station. C'est la Vie!

I have recently been talking to a retired railway engineer who amongst other projects was involved in the construction of the Hong Kong MTR and the Bangkok Airport Rail Link. His opinion was that HS2 would be beneficial as it would relieve congestion on the existing tracks and also open up the possibilty of constructing new lines to link up with towns that had been cut off in the Beeching era.

From Avignon to the junction with the Petit Rhone at Arles was just 35 kilometres and involved one very large lock at Beaucaire which we shared with another huge hotel ship, the Swiss registered "Excellence Rhone," which again filled the entire width of the lock. We moored as far behind it as we could and gave him plenty of time to get away before attempting to follow. If you got too close behind these mighty leviathans you could end up being flung around in the wash like canoeists in the rapids.

We had the joy of another beautiful sunny autumn day with clear blue skies and a fresh airy breeze that whipped up the wash of passing ships into a fine spray. This area can be battered by winds of up to 100 kilometres an hour when the Mistral is in full bore, but this was a fairly gentle and refreshing blow.

After the lock Beaucaire appears on the right bank and Tarasçon, with its imposing fortress- like Medieval castle sits on the opposite side. The two towns are joined by several bridges and actually form one settlement. A few kilometres to the south there is a disused canal that once linked the Rhone with the port of Beaucaire. For some reason this is closed to navigation even though there is a thriving boat harbour in Beaucaire. Rather than a short trip of 18 kilometres boats now have to go via the Petit Rhone to St Gilles and thence to Beaucaire by a roundabout route involving 49 kilometres and one lock! We turned off the Rhone proper into the Petit Rhone which in turn leads to another junction with the Embranchement Canal to Beaucaire. We took this narrow canal as far as the port of St Gilles, our destination for the day.

Looking through the binoculars for a suitable mooring space I immediately recognised the unmistakable outline of the "Tressnish", owned by our old friends John and Judy, and I looked forward to meeting up with them again. Even though we were still a fair distance away I knew instantly that this was Tressnish - I could tell that boat from a mile off! We found a spot on the quay a few boats away from Tressnish and I walked over to say hello. Everything was firmly shut down and there was no sign of life aboard so we adjourned to a nearby cave to stock up with some cheap vino. Early in the evening as we sat on the deck of Pisgah with some chilled vin rosé, a battered Peugeot Estate car came rumbling on to the quay in a cloud of dust and there they were - John and Judy. This amazing bloke had just driven in one stint all the way from Calais. It took poor old John a good five minutes to get himself out of the car, such were the state of his tired old legs, and another five to get over to Pisgah and gratefully accept a glass from Rob. John really never ceased to amaze. He had a terrible joint disorder which was slowly getting worse despite several attempts on the operating table and it had now got so bad that he had to lift his left leg with his hands as it had refused to work by itself. Did this stop John from continuing with his boating? Not one bit. In the boot of his car he'd got a second-hand generator which he intended to install, by himself, in the engine room on Tressnish. How he had intended to get it out I had no idea. It took three of us to manhandle it from the car on to the deck of Tressnish. Once we had lowered it on to the hatch, John said he would be able to get it below with the aid of a small hand-operated winch - the one he used to get his electric scooter on and off the boat. Nothing, it seemed, could deter John and I always marvelled at the way he made light of his extreme disabilities.

"I have a tried and tested way of getting things done if I can't do them myself," he told us. "I go into the nearest bar where there are a few fit young lads, buy them a couple of drinks, and then get them to give me a quick hand to move this *little* generator for me."

Tressnish was moored with the deck level about 6 inches below the quay and he could not get his legs to function enough to climb off the boat without assistance. I sometimes get a tweak in my back or a slight pain in my legs and think the world is coming to an end - what an inspiration John is to everyone. In the evening we all went together for a meal in the town and retired to Tressnish where the four of us polished off a whole bottle of Laphroaig Single Malt, before retiring gracefully (or maybe not so gracefully),to our beds.

Next morning we bade farewell to John and Judy, leaving him to seek out a few willing young lads with strong arms and a penchant for free beer, and headed west once more on the Canal Rhone à Sète. We had an easy 22 kilometre run with just one swing bridge , diverting from the main line canal into the centre of Aigue-Mortes. Mooring here was at a premium but we eventually managed to tie up with the boats rafted together beneath the ancient city walls close to the junction with the Canal Maritime du Grande-Roi, which leads to the Mediterranean Sea. Across on the opposite side of the Grande-Roi was another of Phil Trotter's barges, 'Saul Nomad', owned by a somewhat eccentric character, another John as it happened.

 Saul Nomad had been built at Saul by R W Davis in 2002 and fitted out by Tommy Nielsen at Gloucester Docks. Although we were moored at Saul together for some time I never really got to know John. At that time he owned two massive hairy black dogs - I think they were Newfoundlands, notorious for shedding masses of hair and excessive drooling. Ideal dogs to have on a boat I don't think. During the time that the boat was being built, John would drive to Saul with them in his LWB Land Rover with a camper top and sleep with the bloody things in the car. One of the stories that I heard was that he woke once in the middle of the night with a dry throat, and drank half a pint of water straight from the Gloucester & Sharpness Canal! He apparently lost two stones in as many days - good tip for anyone trying to lose weight - much better than the gym - and it's instant. The crazy thing was that there was a BW drinking-water tap only a few yards from where he was parked!

Saul Nomad was totally hydraulic - engine, gearbox and bow thruster, which I found a bit bizarre. The engine ran at constant revs and the speed was adjusted by using the gearbox - didn't seem right to me and I know he had a few problems with it. Not the least of these was when a pipe split and filled the bilges with gallons of sticky evil-smelling hydraulic fluid.

John didn't exactly endear himself with the "Master", Mr Trotter, by levelling some pretty harsh criticism of the yard on a blog, accusing them of laying the bottom plates on an uneven base. I think it was just as well that John scuttled off to France as soon as he could and kept well out of reach of Saul Junction - and Phil's threat to "twat him straight into the cut".

I cycled over on the Brompton to say hello but there was no sign of him, so I followed the towpath for 10 kilometres towards the sea and the port of Le Grau du Roi.

When I reached the port, the first thing I saw was a sort of Romanesque amphitheatre which, judging by the number of excited people milling around, was putting on some sort of show. Curious to find out what it as all about, I put the bike in "park" mode and eased my way between the columns into the arena. There didn't seem to be any entrance charge and inside was an open air circular sand covered arena surrounded by concrete grandstands, and it wasn't long before the action commenced. The "entertainment" was a strange sort of bullfight - not in the Spanish sense but a sporting event peculiar to the Camargue region of France. The stars of the show here were not the toreadors, or "razeteurs" as they are called, but the bulls themselves, and all the posters advertising the events showed the name of the bulls together with their farm of breeding at the top of the bill. The razeteurs were merely the support act. These animals are trained specifically to take part in these events in which the razeteurs, all dressed in immaculate white shirt and slacks, attempt to capture ribbons and rosettes that are attached to the bulls' horns. Half a dozen or so of these razeteurs run amok around the arena, darting round and round attempting to tire the bull and win the trophies. The bulls enter the ring one at a time through a small gate, and when things get too close for comfort, the razeteurs have to jump the concrete wall into the crowd to escape a pierced buttock and sometimes an over-enthusiastic bull will follow, an action guaranteed to excite the spectators. I kept well away from the wall as you can imagine and thought of a very old joke about a bull called Ferdinand who was corralled in a field adjacent to some rather beautiful cows. One day, after much frustration, he plucked up the courage to jump the barbed wire fence and ravage them. He ran flat out and hurdled the fence. Once across, he sidled rather awkwardly up to the first cow who looked at him doe-eyed and said.

162

"Hi there - you must be Ferdinand the Bull."

"Well," he replied shyly, "you'd better just call me Ferdin. That fence was higher than I thought it was."

Each round lasted about two or three minutes before the bull was shepherded out of the ring to the sound of the aria from Carmen, and the next one led into the ring. The Course Camarguaise, as it known, attracts a knowledgable and impassioned following. The bulls here are not killed and some go on to fight for many years. I couldn't help thinking that it was all a bit cruel to have these animals charging frantically around in the searing heat but I was assured by one avid spectator that this is what they are trained for. I didn't stay too long but I was impressed by the passion of the crowd, enjoying one of the long established traditions of the Camargue. I once witnessed cock fighting in Thailand and I can assure you that was not a pleasant experience. The bullfights, by contrast, were almost tame.

Further on down the canal I came across a different ambience altogether, a canal full of boats flanked by gaily painted stalls and kiosks which opened out into the beautiful and expansive beach and the Mediterranean Sea. I treated myself to a quick dip in the freezing cold ocean and an ice cream before heading back to Aigues-Mortes.

In the evening we walked a few hundred metres into the town and ate a delicious meal of scallops Ste Jacques, soft-shell crab and prawns, beneath the fortified town wall.

Another friend of Rob's, Michel, a flambuoyant local wine wholesaler, joined for a few days and gave us the benefit of some of his knowledge of the vin trade and of his wonderful Mediterranean cooking. As Rob had no space available on Pisgah, Michel bunked in the fore cabin of Saul Trader, and kept us amused with various stories of his exploits in the complex world of the vintner.

As we left the mooring I gave a hoot to Saul Nomad but there was still no sign of life and we re-joined the main canal and turned left to head for Sète and the Étang de Thau. The canal here is wide and straight for 48 kilometres to Sète and hugs the coast quite closely, flanked by several large salt water Étangs (literally translated as "ponds") on both sides, separated by narrow spits of land. For most of the way to the Étang de Thau the Canal has been enlarged to accommodate vessels of up to 1200 tons. One of these, the fully laden "Tennessee" loosed us by with a friendly wave. Shortly after this we encountered an unusual manually operated footbridge at Villeneuve de Maguelone which connects the village with the plage. It actually sits in the water on floats and was opened for us by an operator who had to take many turns of a wheel to let us pass. Shortly after this we passed Frontignan and entered the vast Étang de Thau, following Pisgah in to the channel that led to the port of Sète, where we tied up, breasted together again, on the Quai du Mistral, lakeside of the huge double track bascule railway bridge that carries the busy line from Bordeaux to Marseilles. There are in fact two lifting bascule bridges here, one for the road and one for the railway, and they open for boat traffic twice a day. We looked on as train after train, duble-deck duplex TGV's , 14 coach Inter-Cities and 50 wagon freight trains rumbled across. We were joined by a yacht - mast up - that tied alongside us to await a passage to the sea, complete with the essential fashion accessory, a couple of sun-tanned g-string clad sea nymphs   stretched out on the foredeck.

Sète is a lovely little port, full of boats of all shapes and sizes from sleek expensive ocean-going yachts, to small open day boats and fishing smacks. Naturally there are also some interesting bars along the quays, where sailors in Musto shirts mix with fishermen in smocks and berets to regale yarns of huge catches and terrible storms. Mike and I stopped off in one for a couple of glasses of pression and I noticed that most of the fishermen were smoking: none of the European directive namby pamby nimby pimby for them.

The next day dawned with a fresh breeze that chopped up the waters of the Étang. Saul Trader and Pisgah took it all in their stride as we ploughed westward across the 17 kilometre expanse towards the tiny entrance to the Canal de Midi at Les Onglous. At last we were nearing the ultimate goal. I tried to memorise the channel that we were following for future reference. It is marked with buoys but they are several kilometres apart and quite difficult to make out. There are shallows and a profusion of oyster farms that need avoiding.

After a few kilometres on the Midi we encountered the first two locks, and did not get off to a particularly ideal start. The first shock came when we realised that these Midi locks are a somewhat different shape to any that we had come across before. I suppose we should have been prepared, and I had been vaguely aware of the fact but not given it too much consideration. The sides of these locks are not straight, but rounded, or scalloped, so designed by the builder of the canal, one Pierre Paul Riquet, who opted for the ovoid shape after a wall had collapsed in a conventional straight-sided lock. This posed several problems - not entirely insurmountable problems, but niggling ones nevertheless. The sides of Saul Trader, like all barges, are straight and the shape of the curved sides of the lock made it difficult to secure properly alongside. To make matters worse, the éclusiere at the first lock was a young female student doing holiday work, who didn't have much idea about boating. She insisted that we used two lines, one fore and one aft, but refused to help out by taking them and looping them over the bollards. This, we were to discover, seemed to be policy on the Midi, unlike anywhere else on the French system. Exactly why this was I never discovered, but it didn't make for a very comfortable introduction to the canal. Mademoiselle then insisted that we had to share with not one, but two hire cruisers which had to squeeze in past us to the other side of the lock and then faff about for what seemed an age getting their bits of string sorted out, while she watched unmoved and unmoving. Finally with a defiant stomp to the top of the lock she wound up the paddles full whack which sent torrents of water surging around us, causing one of the hire boat crew to lose grip of the rope which sent them crashing across the lock and into us. To say I went a bit beserk was putting it mildly and probably just as well that the mademoiselle's English didn't extend to the knowledge of four letter obscenities. I shouted at her to lower the paddles but the damage was done. A lesson that made us very wary of Midi locks, and especially female Midi lock-keepers.

After another kilometre we arrived at another quirky wonder of the waterways, the Ecluse Ronde d'Adge, which leads on to the River Herault and the town of Agde, where there are ample moorings adjacent to the lively town that provides a wide choice of eateries and bars. The river widens out towards the port of Le Grau d'Adge, three kilometres away, and the Mediterranean Sea, passing rows of boatyards and chandleries. The circular basin of the lock has two exits. On arrival you need to tell the lock-keeper if you want to turn on to the river or to continue straight ahead. When the lock has emptied you have the choice of heading straight on to the Canal du Midi, or turning left towards the town. I promised myself that one day we would indeed sample the delights of Agde, but for now it was press on regardless. We tied for the night in Michel's home town of Villeneuve les Béziers, some 6 kilometres from Bèziers itself, and by way of a thank you for the trip, Michel treated us all to one of his specialities, a delicious Mediterranean style paella. He had intended to leave for home that night but as a result of a bit more vin (and paella) than anticipated, wisely decided to stay for one more night.

We said our au revoirs in the morning and passed through Bèziers without stopping - we couldn't have stopped even if we had wanted to as there wasn't an inch of mooring space, and after crossing the River Orb on a spectacular aquaduct, headed for another of the seven wonders (there must be at least 27 wonders of the waterways actually), the 9 Écluses Fonseranes - or is it 8? There are in fact 8 pounds and 9 gates although nowadays only 6 locks and 7 gates are used - and of course they are all ovoid shaped. Hope that makes sense!

Once again we had the inconvenience of having to share with a hire boat - this time a completely insane Russian who drove the boat as though it was a Lada in the Moscow rush hour. Crash bang bang bang! As if this wasn't frightening enough, we entered the bottom lock and secured our ropes, to find that the gates of the next two lock were still open. Water was cascading down over the cills like a waterfall from the next closed gate, three chambers ahead of us. My first thought was that we were under the control of another lunatic student who hadn't quite grasped the principle of lock working, but no sooner had Boris and Nikita twisted their strings around the first available solid object they could find, and the top paddles, three lock chambers away, were lifted skywards.

According to Wikipedia, these locks are the third most visited tourist attraction in the Languedoc region, with 320,000 visitors per year. Looking up, I thought that about 300,000 of them had decided to visit that very day. As it happened, it wasn't as disastrous as I had thought it would be. The sight of a mini tidal wave heading towards us at a rate of knots was a bit disconcerting at first, but in the event we were lifted fairly gently up to the next level, so that we could move forward into the next chamber, and so on. Once we had understood the procedure, Mike went ashore and held on to the bow line as we moved from chamber to chamber and in what seemed just a few minutes, we were at the top of the flight. Even Boris had calmed down a bit after I had imparted some friendly words, and only crashed into us three more times! Russia's answer to Timothy West?

There is an interesting water slope adjacent to the locks, in which boats were pushed up by a shield across the channel operated by engines that ran alongside on rails. Unfortunately it was not completed until 1984, long after the demise of most of the commercial traffic, and was soon abandoned due to continual breakdowns and lack of use. That evening we moored in Colombieres, a few hundred metres away from Pisgah and I got a mouthful from a local resident for tying to a tree.

There were a number of narrow low bridges on the Midi and it was not always easy to work out whether we would have enough clearance with the wheelhouse in situ. As the weather was warm and settled, and to be on the safe side, we dismantled it and spent the week cruising al fresco. The guide that I was using showed all the suspect bridge dimensions but of course it was the curve of the arch that made the difference. Some might be higher at the apex but with a narrower arch and others may be wider but lower. I had to do a bit of rudimentary applied mathematics to try to establish which of them might pose a problem. Taking down the wheelhouse wasn't really an issue as we had three or four hands, but with just two it could be difficult. It was usually assumed that the bridge at Capestang was the lowest, although some awarded that honour to the Pont Marengo at the foot of Carcassonne Lock. I reckoned that there were two or three that might prove dodgy - and I marked these with a large asterisk in the guide. There were two factors that needed to be considered - the height at the apex of the arch, and also at the sides where the arch sloped downwards compared with the width of the wheelhouse roof. The wheelhouse on Saul Trader was about 3 metres across at a height of roughly three metres with the boiler chimney removed. The excellent Du Breil guides listed all the lowest bridges together with line drawings which showed the heights at various distances from the centre. Capestang, for example was shown as 3.1 metres height across a width of just 3 metres, so it didn't take a lot to work out that considerable care would be required to get through with the roof in situ. An extra factor was that when the side doors were open they stuck out at an angle from the side and I always tried to remember to close them before attempting to pass. Over the years when we had got more used to them, and when there only two of us aboard, we actually managed to negotiate all of them with the wheelhouse in situ, albeit at a very slow speed and sometimes after two or three aborted attempts.

We were now on the summit of the Canal du Midi, a 50 kilometre lock-free pound, and enjoyed a relaxing cruise with the roof down, bathed in autumn sunshine, to our final destination, Argeliers. It had taken us 12 days from Chalon sur Saone, a distance of 598 kilometres. According to Jules, he had arranged a mooring for us outside a restaurant called "Le Chat Qui Peche", but as is often the case in France, nobody had seemed to communicate the fact with anyone else and when we arrived our promised mooring did not materialise. I think it was taken up with a wreck of a boat that the proprietor of the cafe had been trying to get the owner to remove, without success. Apparently the owner of the restaurant owed Jules some sort of favour but this had not transformed into a mooring. In the event, I tied to a sort of wharf which some said would be OK and others said no way. This was a popular halt for hotel boats and as we had discovered in the past, hotel boats seemed to have their own rules and sod anyone else. Still no hard feelings were apparent and we graced "The Cat That Fishes" for our evening meal and an excellent meal it was. The pork fillet Mignon was superb and I discovered that the French in this part of the world actually chill their red wine. I had been doing this for some time as room temperature on a barge in the heat of a southern French summer almost boiled the wine - something which I could not stomach. In my opinion a lightly chilled glass of red wine is one of the most pleasant and refreshing drinks you could ever have. In Thailand I do the same all the time - and two fingers to any oenophiles who choose to disagree.

Rob did have a mooring sorted out some distance further on at the small village of Ventenac en Minervois, and sailed off the following morning, leaving us to sort ourselves out. In the absence of any alternative, I decided to chance it and leave Saul Trader exactly where it was. They could hardly crane it out and crush it or drill a hole in the bottom and sink it and the worst that could happen was that I would get a nasty letter from the VNF and even possibly a charge, but that wouldn't be the end of the world.

I left the keys with Jules together with a list of jobs to be carried out on Saul Trader over the winter. The main cabin toilet had never functioned properly and the steel shower tray had started to corrode, which in turn had led to the drain hole getting blocked with flaking bits of rusty metal. The wheelhouse woodwork needed a good rub down and a couple of coats of Sikkens as did the pigeon boxes, and the roof canvas also needed repainting and weatherproofing. Jules had a number of contacts in the trade and assured me that he could get these jobs sorted out before the spring.

Aigues - Mortes

Railway bascule bridge at Séte

Chapter 10   Sur le Midi

I returned with Joe and Mary the following May. We crossed the Channel on the LD Lines ferry route from Portsmouth to Le Havre. The advantage of this was that as the ship left Portsmouth at 11 o'clock in the evening and timed its arrival at Le Havre for 8.00 am the next morning, you could get a reasonable night's kip by booking a cabin and arrive fresh and ready for the long drive south. We had a couple of drinks in the bar and leant on the rail as we steamed past the few warships that we still possessed in the naval dockyard, and the lights of Southsea front on our port side as we made our way into the Solent, and retired to our cabins just after midnight. I turned the key in the door of my designated cabin and opened it to be greeted with a muffled scream and the sight of a woman cowering in the top bunk, covering her modesty with a sheet. I think we were both equally shocked and I quickly shut the door muttering something about bloody LD Lines and headed for the Bureau. The Purser was most apologetic and gave me another key. He couldn't understand how the mistake had occurred and I suggested that he go immediately to explain to the unfortunate woman what had happened and assure her that I wasn't intent on robbing her, or at worse, a potential rapist! As I sat eating breakfast the next morning the woman came and spoke to me - not sure how she recognised me to be honest - but I bought her a cup of coffee and we both had a bit of a laugh about it.

We took the "fast" route from Paris via the A71/ A75. Through the tunnels of Paris we dodged the motor bikes around the Periphique, making sure we kept well to the left of the lane so that they could undertake us on the "wrong" side, hazards lights blinking as though they could ensure the safety of their riders. You would certainly get some looks-that could-kill if you forgot this unwritten rule and unwittingly blocked their path. Once through the congested Parisian suburbs we had a reasonably clear run on the autoroute to the south.

I had got myself one of the little magic sensors from Sanef, the people who administered the autoroutes, which meant that I could now use the express lanes through the toll booths, something that Fergus could well have done with. It was just a small plastic disc that attached to the windscreen and sent a signal to the barrier control, which raised the barrier automatically. Until recently the only way you could sign up for this was by having a French bank account, but this had now been extended to include British ones. It was a very convenient way to travel - no more queueing for a ticket. At the other end when you came to leave the autoroute, the same procedure applied - into the express lane and no sooner had you passed through, your bank account was relieved of the requisite amount of Euros for the privilege. It was a bit nerve-wracking for the first few times. Would it recognise us and open or would we have the embarrassing situation hilariously described by Ferg? The trick was to approach at exactly 30 kilometres per hour which would mean you could drive through without even stopping. It was a bit like a Formula 1 drive-through penalty, the slight difference being that you weren't getting paid a million dollars for it. The best part of the whole process was seeing the faces of the " under-privileged " as they queued up to fiddle with their credit cards or work out how to pay. You would sometimes get a raised eyebrow from some know-it-all (usually a French man) that said "look at this idiot foreigner in the wrong lane - this should be fun", at which point you put your foot down and gleefully speed away into the distance.

It was also amusing to see the faces of drivers who had overtaken us several kilometres before the toll when they suddenly realised that they were having to pass you all over again. I was overtaken by some flash "gent" in a Range Rover with blackened windows and a pathetic personal registration - something ridiculous that he had probably paid several grand

Deluge at Écluses Fonserannes

The Bassin Ronde

for - like P111 OCK - which he had tried unsuccessfully to doctor so that it read "P.L.Lock" , which presumably was his name - bit careless if he was a gangster, or a drug baron, but actually looked more like Pillock. I saw one in the States once, where you could buy any combination of letters, that obviously belonged to one Robert Soul. He had chosen, after careful deliberation, the registration plate R.SOUL! Anyway, Pillock had overtaken us doing well over a ton a few kilometres from the approaching toll booth. I watched as he joined the back of a mile long queue while I slid nonchalantly over to the fast-track lane, slowed to 30, got the green light as the barrier rose, and accelerated away, narrowly beating Lewis Hamilton's last pit-stop time. Mr P finally caught up with us again about 10 kilometres further on , giving us a suspicious-looking stare as he flashed past.

This superb motorway affords some wonderful scenic panoramas as it passes through the mountains of the Massif Central. We stopped at the next rest area, for a quick coffee and to take a look at the Cabaret bridge, a magnificent cast iron railway viaduct built by Eiffel in 1885. It is over 500 metres long and spans the Truyere river valley at a height of 125 metres. As we pulled up in the car park "Pillock" appeared from the gents, zipping up his trousers. Seeing us again he sauntered across and gestured for me to wind down my window.

"'Ow'd you do that then?" he demanded, "get in front like that eh."

I was reluctant to divulge my secret and mumbled something about being lucky to have found a shorter queue. I'm not sure he was that convinced but nevertheless turned and walked away with a desultory grunt, jumped into the drug-dealer-mobile and roared off.

A few kilometres further south there is what must rank as one of the seven wonders of the motorways, if there is such a thing, the quite spectacular Viaduc de Millau, the tallest bridge in the World. It is two and a half kilometres long and spans the River Tarn at a height of 270 metres above the ground. It was designed by our very own Norman Foster and opened in 2004. There is a fantastic breath-taking view of the entire bridge on the approach from the north as it appears in the distance. The many bridges and viaducts and amazing views of the landscape make this one of the most interesting motorways to drive on anywhere in France, and help to relieve the tedium of a long journey.

Just before Béziers the heavens opened! I think we must have had the whole months' worth of rain dumped on us in the next hour and a half. It bounced in the roads and flooded the drainage system and caused us to slow down to fifty kilometres an hour. I had recently acquired a Land Rover Discovery, and this was its maiden voyage and I have to say that I had never experienced a vehicle better equipped to cope with the conditions. The car took it all in its stride and ploughed through with a consummate leisurely ease. When we finally arrived at Argeliers it was dark and there was no sign of Saul Trader anywhere near the mooring where we had left it. I called Jules who said that it had been moved a hundred yards or so up the towpath. He still had the key but as he was about to take a shower we would have to collect it from his house. That was the first problem. Although I had been there before it was in daylight and I couldn't quite remember the way. Jules gave me some sparse directions and after about half an hour and a few wrong turns we managed to find it again. Jules and Jess were going out for the evening and he was obviously in a hurry. He threw me the keys and told me he would come down to see us in the morning. The next thing was to find the boat. The rain was still coming down in spades and the towpath was rapidly looking much like a very muddy ploughed field. The Disco came into its own now as I selected a suitable off road mode and we slithered through the trees in the direction that Jules had told us they had taken the boat. The mud was a foot deep in places and at times the track was a bit too close to the edge of the canal for comfort. Jules' 100 yards turned out nearer to three hundred before we picked out the stern of Saul Trader in the headlights. I didn't relish the prospect of six mud-caked boots trampling over the deck so I suggested going aboard first to get some lights on and put some old mats down outside the wheelhouse door. I manoeuvred the car as close to the boat as possible with the headlights helping to illuminate my path, cursing the lovely Jules under my breath.

Saul Trader was moored about three feet out beside an uneven bank which was now quite treacherously wet and slippery. I managed to get aboard with a bit of a stretch and get the door open before taking off my boots which were by now plastered with mud. I tiptoed down below into the engine room and threw the master switches to turn on the power - and nothing, absolutely nothing! I knew the domestic batteries were getting towards the end of their life and we had six new ones in the car, but in these conditions, wet and dark, there was no way we were going to be able to get them on to the boat, let alone connected. Apart from anything else it was getting on for 10 o'clock and we were all pretty knackered. I tried the genny but its battery was also as dead as a dodo. I laid out a couple of mats in the doorway and conveyed the good news to Jo and Mary. We did at least have gas and we had a few bottles of water and some wine that I had bought on the ferry so it could have been worse. I lit the two emergency Camping Gaz lanterns, Mary put the kettle on and I opened a bottle of Cab Sauv - things started to look up! It's surprising just how quickly you can adapt to situations like this. We'd lived through the power cuts and the miner's strikes and the three day weeks. True we'd never had to endure quagmired trenches whilst being bombarded with enemy shells, but we had been through hard-ish times - and Jo and Mary were hardy types. So we settled down in the cosy gloom with our coffee and wine and after a couple of glasses were more than ready for bed. The problems would just have to wait until the morning.

We all slept pretty well in the circumstances and I was up early in the morning and had the coffee brewing by 7 o'clock. The rain had stopped but I could hardly say it was a bright spring morning. There were dark clouds and the temperature was definitely on the cool side for May in the south of France. We broke our fasts on some stale croissants that Mary had kept from the previous day and set about getting the boat into some sort of an operational state. The first thing to do was to sort out the power and I disconnected all the old batteries, having first drawn up a diagram showing the connections. There were six

110 ah domestic batteries and they needed to be connected in the correct order to avoid blowing up the whole shebang! Things like "in parallel" or "in series" come to mind and I hadn't much idea what each one meant - or did. They were bloody heavy too and it was quite a job getting the old ones off and the new ones on to the boat, especially when the decks were so far away from the slippery bank, but we managed it, luckily without dropping any in the cut, and after a couple of hours, we were ready to give them a try.   And oh what joy! With a flick of the master switch we had light, we had pumps, we had functioning toilets <u>and</u> we had that wondrous magic of the white man - Electricity. The next thing on the list was to clean the boat of all the tree debris and gunge that had accumulated over the winter. I started the engine and Jo and I set to with the deck wash and brushes. By lunchtime we were both soaked through and the boat was looking good again.

The work done by Julian and his men over the winter looked OK and for the first time in 13 years we had a proper loo in the master cabin - a bit on the noisy side, but at least it did the job of disposing its contents into the holding tank and re-filling the bowl with water from the cut. Luxury indeed!   The woodwork on the wheelhouse and pigeon boxes shone like new and the wheelhouse roof had been weatherproofed with a couple of coats of canvas paint. The steel shower tray in the master cabin, that had started to rust quite badly, had been completely cleaned and painted with a waterproof sealant. Safari so goodee - until I went to have a shower in the evening and the first snag became apparent. In their enthusiasm for the paint job, they had obviously forgotten that the drain hole was exactly that, a drain hole, and needed to be kept clear.They had forgotten to cover it and it had blocked up stopping the water from draining away. I pointed out the problem to Jules when he arrived and a quick call ensured that the gang was on the job within the hour and after a bit of persuasion with the rods the blockage was cleared.

While we were washing the decks I had noticed that the engine was running hot and I put this down to muck in the mud box. This happened periodically, especially when we had moored in shallow water close to an un-piled bank, and it was a simple job to take out and clean the mud filter. However when I got it out, I found that it was clear and definitely not the cause of the problem this time. I checked the water levels and restarted the engine but there was very little water passing through the system. The next thing to check was the impeller. I still had the spare one that I bought after the last one failed on the Kennet & Avon 10 years ago. As luck would have it, some friends of Jo and Mary, who had moved to France and were living an hour or so from Argelier, were coming to visit.

Chris and Christine (Chrissie) arrived just in time as I was peering into the hole where the impeller was situated, firmly wedged and seemingly impossible to remove. Chris is another of those practical types, who may not necessarily have the specific knowledge but who have the analytical engineering mind and the determination not to be beaten by some inanimate object, however bloody-minded and awkward it may prove to be. Chris immediately warmed to the challenge. Within minutes of his arrival he was on his hands and knees in the engine room and in less than an hour he'd got the old one off - it only had two of its twelve blades still intact - and the new one fitted. We were in business at last and all at once the weather started brightening!

The pound, or bief partage, that stretches from the top of the Fonserrannes flight of locks at Beziers, all the way to the bottom of the lock at Argens, provides lock free boating for 54 kilometres, Christmas and Birthday all in one for the lazy lock-fearing boater. We left Argeliers at the end of May 2012, and didn't venture any further west than Toulouse, the western limit of the Midi, until the end of July 2013. It is easy to get lazy canal boating on this stretch. I have to say that I usually get itchy feet after a couple of days moored in the same place, but I can quite understand those who having found their ideal spot, get more and more reluctant to disconnect the umbilical cord and leave the security of familiarity to cast off into the unknown.

Over the next months several friends came for a week or so break and we found ourselves visiting the same places again and again. It was quite relaxing and of course the summer climate of the south of France contributed to the laid back shorts-and-flip-flop lethargy. We jury-rigged a canopy for the fore-deck and spent the evenings fending off the mosquitos whilst playing cribbage and indulging ourselves with large amounts of chilled vin rosé and seafood salad. Our first day took us back to Capestang. I was still not sure about the clearance at the bridge and we nosed up to it before chickening out and mooring on a rickety pontoon just outside the harbour. One benefit of this was that it was free and still just a short walk into the main square, where we found an excellent restaurant in the corner, the Café de la Grille. Another useful feature of French life is the opening hours of the shops. Most close during the afternoon so that their owners can digest their somewhat indulgent lunch, but then open again until late in the evening. Once you get used to this anomaly it is a simple matter of reorganising your shopping habits to suit. The little tube that I had labelled as "Betty Swollocks" had run dry and the irritating little rash had reappeared so a replenishment was called for. I found a small pharmacy just off to the side of the square where a bright young man, who I assumed had recently qualified in the trade and spoke excellent English, understood my requirement immediately after my Basil Fawlty "dragonfly" performance, pointing at the offending part of my body and making frenzied scratching movements accompanied by a few ooohs and aaahs.

"OK, no problem," he said, raising his eyebrows as if to add "just explain the problem - no need for the theatrics thank you" and bending down to fetch a small tube from under the counter with a flourish. " It is how do you say .... I have forgotten the word .... oh our, yes .....it is the mushroom ? - you have the mushrooms.?"

It took me a few moments to realise what it was he meant before the penny dropped.

"Fungus," I suggested, "we call it a fungus."

"Ah bien sur, of course, a fungus," he said and we both laughed out loud.

The first thing I did, after applying some of the medication to the delicate area, was to mark the box. I didn't want to be using it on a gum boil! The dilemma was whether to stick to my tried and tested method or label the box "Mushrooms."

There is a hire company based here that as well as the ubiquitous plastic bumper car noddy boats, also have a few Linnssen steel cruisers available for hire. These are built in Maasbracht on the Meuse in Holland and rank amongst the best (well certainly the most expensive) on the market. They are usually the preserve of rich and haughty Dutchmen who rather think that owning one gives them automatic rights and priority over anyone else on the cut. They tie up with gaps between them which they vehemently defend from gate-crashers until one of their own - another Dutchman with another shiny Linnssen arrives, when they shift up to make room as if by magic, and put their towels on the lock gates at 6 o'clock in the morning to ensure that they get through before anyone else when the lock opens at 9 o'clock. The ones that are hired at Capestang look to all intents and purposes like the "real" thing as they aren't emblazoned with company logos, and so it is easy to make the mistake that the one coming towards you will be skippered by a large Hollander with his fat wife wielding a boat hook standing on the bow like Boadicea ready to attack anyone daring to come within 12 yards of their precious lump of metal. It always makes for some amusement when the little boat rears off sideways and rams the bank in panic and you realise that it is just another hire boatee with probably about three hours experience of handling anything that floats and has probably been practising with a plastic toy tug in the bath.

Next morning we executed a pretty neat three point turn with just a few feet clearance from the bank in front of the errant bridge and a few spectators before retracing our steps back through Argeliers. There is a long straight before the small Port la Robine and the entrance to the Canal de Jonction to Narbonne and the sea. Along the straight section there is a self-check speed zone - not with towpath radar guns or cameras, or signs warning that there could well be a gendarme hiding in the bushes with a gun, (2746 motorists prosecuted this week), but simply two boards 1300 metres apart. If you pass between them in less than ten minutes you are basically going too fast. The speed limit is 8 kilometres per hour, and it doesn't take a mathematician to work out that 1.33 kilometres should take you a minimum of 10 minutes - 6 times 1.33 equals 7.98, or at least it did in the old days when I was at school- not that we had ever heard of metres when I was at school, but there you are. It never really applied to us on Saul Trader as even when we had plenty of water under us we would be hard pressed to make 6 kph, but it was amusing to watch some of the hire boaters (and it has to be said, some private boats too) veering from side to side as their skippers checked their watches and tried desperately to activate the calculator app on their mobile phones, while their boat headed flat out for the bank. Amongst the line of moored boats just after the port we found the 'Tressnish' and John and Judith and we tied alongside for half an hour for a cup of tea and a catch up on the news. John had been moored at Saul for several years and so we had a few mutual acquaintances that we could gossip about in their absence. They told us that some of the boaters were organising a barbecue in a couple of days and we resolved to try to get back for it. Shortly after the moorings there is an aqueduct that takes the canal across the somewhat unfortunately named River Cesse, where there is a small café and souvenir shop before the canal turns left on a very tight bend. And that very tight bend was where we encountered our first Canal du Midi hotel boat, smack in the middle of the cut, all 30 metres of longeur and 5 metres of largeur, with very little room to manoeuvre. This resulted in a delicate nautical move, or a slamming on of the anchors in road vehicle parlance. I quickly decided that the Rosa would be better suited to the outside of the bend, and in the non-availability of the blue board, which had been carefully stowed in the forward hold since Holland, I had to resort to another tried and tested nautical signal, a frantic wave of the arm to indicate "you go that side." The captain of the Rosa, a jolly man of African descent, stood at the huge wheel beaming broadly underneath a large Panama hat and skillfully guided his ship around the outside of Saul Trader without touching the sides. We got to know Marco quite well over the next couple of years, through more close encounters of the barging kind, and he always greeted us with that same beaming smile and a tip of his outsize hat - a lovely guy who obviously enjoyed his job in spite

181

of the pressures of keeping his passengers happy and his ship afloat. No mean task in the shallow and narrow Canal du Midi and one that demanded constant concentration. One thing for sure, it was far better to be passing hotels boats going in the opposite direction than to be lumbered having to follow one, doing about 1.25 kph and stuck out of necessity in the very middle of the cut with absolutely no room to overtake.

We found one of these not very far ahead. Having safely negotiated our way past the Rosa and entertained the ice-cream sucking gongoozlers that were sitting under umbrellas outside the café, we were soon approaching the small hamlet of Le Somail, where we stopped for lunch. There are a number of very good restaurants here, a floating grocery shop based on a converted peniche where you can pre-order your baguette by telephone and collect it as you pass almost without stopping: a sort of canal-based "RAS" exercise - or should it be "ROC" - refuelling on cut - or even a drive-through MacDonalds perhaps. There's an incredible antiquarian bookshop stacked high to the rafters with everything from rare first editions to Mills & Boon romantic paperbacks - and another tricky little bridge which needs some very careful negotiation, not least as there is a busy restaurant right beside it where the clientele pay extra for the cabaret to sit outside expectantly awaiting a disaster!

Our disaster came, not from passing though the bridge, which we accomplished very very slowly but without incident, but with the sudden appearance of the dreaded scenario of a hotel barge ahead, going in the same bloody direction as us. The "Langon" had overtaken us as we were just about to untie our ropes and set off - and it was full of over excited schoolboys who were each being given a turn on the wheel by the attractive young lady skipper.

Quel dommage Rodney!

As it happened, we were only moving some 4 kilometres further on to Ventenac en Minervois, where Rob was holed up on Pisgah, but it took the best part of three hours, the canal twisting and turning, and us gazing alternately at the stern of the Langon and the stern of the lady skipper. There's not very much at Ventenac to be honest, although a number of ex-pat

Brits have settled there in some of the newly built bungalows that are set on the bank overlooking the canal. You would certainly need some form of transport if staying for any length of time as the nearest town of any size is Ginestas which is about three kilometres away. Ventenac does have a couple of very good canalside restaurants, a small hut that opens for bread and a sprinkling of groceries for four hours each morning, and a wine cave, adjacent to the canal with a restored wine barge moored at the quay outside. There is also an excellent poubelle or rubbish facility that provides options for all varying types of rubbish which once deposited in the relevant bin, crash down into an underground tank. These are emptied at least once a week. Why are we so far behind the times with everything we do in good old not-so-great Britain?

There was a line of bank-side moorings with no water or electricity facilities, and we found Rob tied up to a tree. Well, that's not quite accurate. He was on his boat which was tied to a tree. We breasted up to Pisgah but Rob warned us that we would probably have to move because the hotel boats would not be able to pass each other in the space outside of us. I was getting increasingly concerned about all the do's and don'ts gradually raising their ugly heads on the Midi. Why was it so different from the laissez-faire approach everywhere else in France with all these petty restrictions? I knew that finding a mooring might be difficult but I had been assured by Jules that we would be able to find somewhere: so far nothing had materialised. Rob had tucked himself nicely into the bank and had already negotiated a supply of electricity and water for a small monthly fee from a nearby house. I was still out on a limb and began to worry about finding anywhere to leave the boat for the winter. We did have a few months to look though so for the time-being we would just bumble around and keep our eyes open. Jules suggested that we speak to the VNF manager who was based in the town of Sallèles d'Aude on the Canal de Jonction, so the next move would be in that direction. We stayed in Ventenac for a few nights and sampled the excellent moules and the scallops accompanied with more than our fair share of pichers of vin rosé in the Grillade de Chateau in a friendly atmosphere orchestrated by David, the eccentric comedian of a waiter. On the second afternoon we took Rob's car and drove back to Port Robine for John and Judith's barbecue.

They had set up some long tables on the towpath next to the aqueduct over the river Cesse and we had a lively time with about a dozen bargees who were living on their assorted vessels along the bank. We met a young couple who we got to know as friends over the next few years. Seppe, a Belgian and his chatty girlfriend, Diwi, who came from the Netherlands. They were travelling the canals on their beautiful Dutch 28 metre Clipper, Johanna, which Seppe was gradually transforming into a comfortable, if somewhat basic, floating home. We also met their crazy friend Wilbur, who favoured T shirts that were more hole than fabric, and who lived on a small wooden yacht. We learned that Wilbur was an unlikely world renowned authority on telescopes, wrote papers on the subject, and travelled the world lecturing to fellow observers. They were all going for a dip in a deep pool on the river below and we joined them for a cool refreshing swim, trying to put out of our minds that we were in fact bathing in the "cesse".

The wine flowed, the steaks were tender and the evening warm and balmy. I too was beginning to warm a little more to the delights of the Canal du Midi. There was also another odd couple, or should I say, triple, who lived on a converted peniche, the top of which was completely covered in solar panels. They were all in their early eighties and apparently there was one man, an Austrian and two elderly sisters, and they all shared the same bed. The mind boggles, but then whatever turns you on! The boats and the people living afloat at Port Robine illustrated a small capsule of a waterborne community of drop-outs and characters tired of normal lives. I must say I found a certain affinity with them and maybe even briefly envied their simple uncomplicated lives, and I know that Joe and the lovely ageing hippy Mary, would have given anything to join them, but we had to get back to reality and the now, for better or worse.

So with that in mind we retraced our steps the following day back through the little bridge at Le Somail that seemed to get smaller each time we approached, passing our new-found

184

friends at Port Robine with a hoot and a wave, before turning right on to the Canal de Jonction towards Sallèles d'Aude. There are five downhill locks that lead the canal to the small basin at Sallèles which I think were put in for the benefit of anyone suffering lock withdrawal symptoms. They are boater operated but entail one crew member going ashore to operate the controls which are set into consoles on the lock-sides. They are all relatively close together which means that you can leave your lock-wheeler ashore for the duration, to go ahead and prepare each lock in turn, either on foot or better still, by fold-up velo. At Sallèles there are a few quayside moorings close to the centre of the little town. There is a large Casino supermarket a kilometre or so from the basin, a bar and a tabac, which usually has a few day old English newspapers in stock, and a small oil depot that will deliver fuel to your boat by tanker. A few years ago there was a move by the local Maire to turn the place into a haven for the gay and lesbian community, and a gay village - apparently the first of its kind anywhere in the world, was even given planning consent, but I think the idea was abandoned after some vehement objections from the existing "straight" population. We found the VNF office beside the next lock but it was firmly shuttered and barred. A call to the number given in the guide also went unanswered so we adjourned to the bar, run by a couple of gays, for a beer and a flick through yesterday's Telegraph.

The next morning there was still no sign of life from the office, so we took the opportunity for a stroll along the canal towards Narbonne. I particularly wanted to have a look at the connection with the Canal de Jonction and the Canal de Robine which involved a short but somewhat tricky crossing of the River Aude. The last lock before the river section is at Gailhousty - God knows how the French pronounce it but it looks more Scottish than French to me. The lock is quite unique and well worth a visit in its own right. It is in fact a double lock staircase, but with a ledge alongside the lower chamber that serves as a dry dock.

For normal passage the middle gate is left open and the lock treated as one, albeit with the chamber twice the length. Boats wishing to use the dry dock, and there is a very long waiting list for it as I discovered, must use the lock as a double staircase. Having dropped down the top chamber to the middle level, the boat has to be manoeuvred to the side of the lower chamber and as the the water is emptied the boat will come to rest on blocks, high and dry, some 6 feet above the lower water level. Ingenious - and I am amazed that the method wasn't used more often. We chatted to the owner of a small tjalk that was having her bottom scrubbed. He was full of praise for the facility - there was water and electricity available, but his one problem was the lack of any cover. This meant that he had to suffer in the searing heat and had jury-rigged a temporary canvas sheet that could be adjusted to cover the working area relevant to the position of the sun. I think if would also cause a bit of consternation if the heavens opened just as you had finished your second coat of tar. On the opposite side of the lock there is another interesting building that houses a museum dedicated to a Roman pottery that produced large terracotta urns, or amphora, between the 1st and 3rd Centuries AD, that were used to transport Narbonne wine to Rome. The museum has displays of the ovens and draining basins, the water used by the potters being brought to the factory on an aqueduct, which is preserved in excellent condition after almost 2000 years. There are models of the original plant and examples of the amphora, and replica thatched roofed houses that were homes to the potters.

There was also a single track railway branch line that was built specifically to transport wine to Narbonne. It was opened in 1887 and connected the town of Bize with the main line at Narbonne. Over the years until its closure in 1939 the railway carried rice, grain, flour and animal feed in addition to the wine, and in 1905 35000 passengers were recorded passing through the station at Sallèlles which is still intact and has recently been the subject of some renovation. The track is still all in situ: the French do not immediately rip up track and sell it off for scrap or allow building over closed trackbeds, unlike the good old British, and it wouldn't take too much to get the line running again. It did enjoy a brief renaissance from 1983 to 2004 when a single preserved railcar operated on the line for tourists. It would make for an excellent attraction and bring some much needed trade to the area and I really hope that someday we will see it running once again - with steam, or maybe that is too much to hope for!

It was difficult to get near to the river Aude as the banks were densely overgrown, so I never managed to see the area of the river that would have to be negotiated when making the trip to Narbonne. We did discover the "niceities" of the crossing, to our cost, some years later. No matter, we weren't going to be doing it on this trip anyway. Joe and Mary had pressing matters to attend to back in blighty - something called work I think it was - ah yes I remember that - nasty little four letter word!

The VNF madame was still noticeable by her absence, so I decided to leave Saul Trader exactly where it was for a few weeks to see whether this triggered any response. As usual, I left a sheet in the window with details of my UK number en cas d'urgence. It obviously had the desired effect as when I returned five weeks later there it was. Slapped on to the side window of the wheelhouse and secured with half a roll of wide beam heavy duty sellotape - the summons. Well not that sort of summons - this wasn't the Canal & River Trust we were dealing with here who would have had you jailed and banned from the cut for life for less. No - this was the much more benign and user-friendly VNF, the Voies Navigables de France. Madame la Chef requesting the pleasure of my attendance at her office at my earliest convenience. All very nice and polite but with one small problem. The bloody office was still locked, bolted and barred. After a more thorough perusal of the notice, once I had managed to prise it off the window without cracking the glass, I saw that madame had pencilled a telephone number in the bottom corner. It was a mobile and one that I hadn't previously tried. It was my invitation to the inner sanctum, the very bosom, of Madame la Chef.

And what a bosom it turned out to be - the sort that projected menacingly outward - conveying the distinct message of "don't mess with me! " As it happened, Madame Trompier - please call me Michelle, was a very smart and attractive middle aged lady who seemed much too nice to be in such an authoritative position. I explained my predicament and she told me that

187

there was absolutely no space available for the winter in Sallèles d'Aude, but Ventenac might be a possibility. She peered at her papiers over the top of her spectacles and smiled. "I think I can find somewhere for you at Ventenac. If you can meet me there at 4 o'clock on Thursday afternoon I will show you the place. You are able to transfer the money by the bank?" My first thought that she was suggesting that I stuff Euros into a brown paper bag and leave them under a tree on the canal bank, but then I realised the sort of Bank to which she was referring.

"Yes of course," I told her and she took out another form for me to fill in with the details of my Bank. When all was duly signed and sealed I took my leave and cast off to reverse back some 100 yards or so to the winding hole and start the climb, single-handed, back up the five locks to the junction with the Midi. It took me five hours for the 13 kilometres and 5 locks, about 15 lock/kilometres, so about 3 per hour - not too bad considering that I had to get off the boat at each of the lock landings to empty the lock, and then climb the ladder from the boat in each lock to set the operation in motion. I always threw a line ashore in these situations, as much as anything to hold the boat close in to the wall. As sod would have it I didn't pass a single boat from the opposite direction until I had just set the very last one.

Back at Ventenac I met up with Robert and we spent a pleasant couple of hours on his newly installed decking (I told him it would only take a few potted shrubs and it would look just like his back garden) on the stern of Pisgah. The moorings at Ventenac looked out over some fantastic views to the south, across the Aude valley to the distant Pyrenees, still sporting a light dusting of snow on the peaks, and we watched an orange ball of sun sink behind the mountains in the west as we finished the first bottle of Vin Rosé, with the smell of garlic prawns gently emanating from the sawn off oil drum that served as the barbecue. Thursday 4 o'clock came and went with no sign whatsoever of the lovely Michelle - shame really as I had wasted an expensive amount of aftershave for the occasion. I found a satisfactory space with enough water to float my boat and tied up to some trees . This was a luxury that was soon to be lost as the spread of the dreaded canker stain that was gradually killing off the iconic and much photographed avenues of plane trees meant that thousands of them were being cut down. A massive campaign by the VNF has seen thousands of replacement saplings of a hardier variety planted in their place and it is hoped that before too long, this unique aspect of the Midi, essential for shade and shelter from the wind and home to a million noisy crickets, will be restored to its former beauty.

Over the next few weeks I bimbled around the area, sometimes on my own and at other times accompanied by friends on weekly trips from the UK. This gave me an excuse to revisit places and we watched the Bastille Day celebrations and fireworks with Dave and Becky from the bridge at Capestang - I still hadn't plucked up the courage to go through. We nosed the bow under it again but then discretion (or was it panic) took over and we backed out on to our usual mooring spot. We dived down the 5 locks to Salléles where I took the opportunity to replenish the tanks with 600 litres of derv delivered by the local tanker. I did manage to find Michelle - no explanation about her non-appearance at Ventenac was offered - and asked her whether I could leave ST in the port again and she readily agreed. Saul Trader was now "official" with its own fully paid up membership, part of the establishment. Actually that wasn't quite true. Although I had signed the forms to set up a direct debit to pay for the mooring, no money had yet been transferred. In fact I left the boat at Ventenac for almost nine months over that winter and never got charged a single cent.

I did another single-handed run to the western end of the level pound and ventured up the the 5 locks that can cause delays in busy periods (one single and two double lock staircases) to the little town of Homps, a former commercial port that was used to transport the excellent local wines to Bordeaux. There are two large marina basins, one of which provides a base for the Le Boat hire company, and more restaurants than are good for it. The first night's mooring is free of charge and includes electricity - an enterprising way to encourage boaters to make use of the facilities in the town and more importantly to spend a few Euros! There is also an excellent store situated just a short walk from the quay that among others things usually has a couple of Daily Telegraphs in stock.

There are several aquaducts that carry the canal over a number of small streams. One in particular, which suddenly appears after an extremely tight bend at Paraza and crosses the river Repudre, is worthy of a mention as it was built by the original architect of the Canal du Midi, Monsieur Riquet himself, and was reputedly the first ever built in France. Riquet lived nearby in the Paraza Chateau which along with its vineyards and cellars, can be visited today and samples of the produce acquired in exchange for cash. On the way back to Ventenac I stopped below the bottom lock at Argens in a quiet rural spot on a warm and sunny evening. There was one other boat some way ahead of me and I began to sift through my meagre supply of rations to rustle up some sort of dinner. A gentleman wandered down the towpath and introduced himself as Ted from Leeds. We exchanged the usual boater pleasantries and I invited him aboard for a glass. Ted was with his wife Judith on the wooden cruiser that was moored ahead and after an hour or so of chat and a couple more glasses, he obviously took pity on me and asked me back to the boat for dinner. I thought it a little rash of him to make the offer without consulting the memsahib but he assured me that they were having curry and that there was plenty of it. I arrived at their boat with a couple of bottles at 8.00pm and it was after midnight when I finally stumbled my way back to Saul Trader after an excellent meal accompanied with some good old-fashioned Yorkshire company. I did refrain from reeling out any of my Yorkshire jokes, however, and we vowed to meet up again and I promised, somewhat rashly that I would do the cooking next time round. In the light of this it was probably fortunate for them that our paths never crossed again. Ships that pass in the night.

Moored at Ventenac en Minervois

Bucolic mooring for Pisgah

Pretty canalside hamlet of La Somail

Bit breezy on the Étang du Thau

Despite my use of the Mark Twain quote at the beginning of this book, all of these stories are true and really did happen.
All of the characters are real too and are people that have been important to me as friends for many years and have greatly enriched my life. Thank you to all of you.
One or two names have been changed, however, to protect the idiot!
As somebody once said, "there's one in every village! "

With grateful thanks to all those who accompanied me on these trips for putting up with me and adding to the quality of the experience with their humour and knowledge and the bonus of their company.

Particular thanks to Allen Maslen for his input and encouragement - a legend and an inspiration.Allen has written several interesting books which can also be found on Kindle.

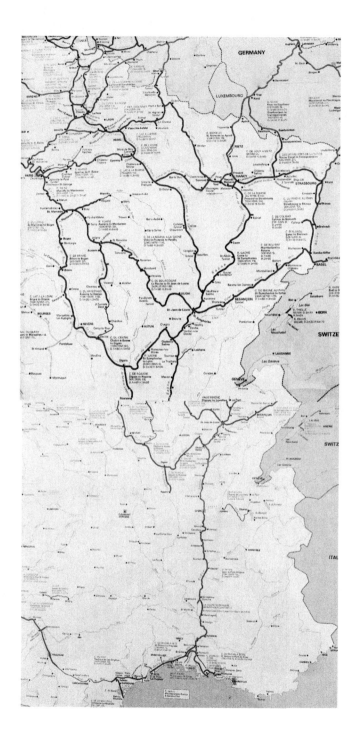

Author Page

I was born and brought up in Hastings, beside the sea, and many miles from the nearest navigable canal.

It was not until 1976 that we hired our first narrowboat from North Kilworth and spent a week circumnavigating the Midlands. I was immediately hooked.

I had always had a keen interest in railways and the canals held the same fascination for me.

I bought my first narrowboat in 1984 and got the chance to add the replica Dutch Luxemo

tor barge to the "fleet", in 1998. I still have both boats and I still get the same "kick" when I go aboard after an absence.

The lore of the Cut has stayed with me and will do so as long as I live.

Keith Harris

www.keithharrisauthor.com

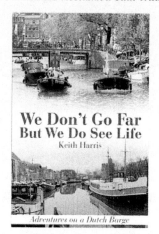
Available from Mortons Books (www.mortonsbooks.co.uk

Or from my website (www.keithharrisauthor.com)

We Don't Go Far but We Do See Life

This is the first of a series of four books that follow the voyages of the Dutch barge 'Saul Trader' from the River Severn in Gloucestershire to Bordeaux in the South West corner of France. Stories of the people and the places, the ups and the downs of travel on a barge around Europe, told with a liberal helping of tongue-in-cheek and enlivened with a fair smattering of anecdote and humour. We navigate the sometime treacherous waters of the Severn Estuary and drag the bottom of the Kennet & Avon Canal to the River Thames and London, before braving the busy shipping lanes of the English Channel to reach France. We suffer the first of several flooded bilges, climb through the four Belgian boat lifts and get serenaded at a music festival, dodge the massive ships in the water motorways of Holland and enjoy the spectacle of the Dordrecht in Steam weekend, before savouring the delights and dangers of Amsterdam to Friesland along smaller more typical Dutch waterways , lockless and lined with windmills. Finally we return to France after a hairy passage of the turbulent Albert Canal and the excitement of the Ronquierres Plane and brand new Strepy-Thieu boat life, to winter in Cambrai.

  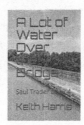
All available from y website (keithharrisauthor.com)

Or at Amazon.co.uk

We'll Cross that Bridge When We Go Under It

In the second book we venture from Cambrai back into Belgium and the Chantier Naval boatyard at Namur.

Then to Paris via the River Meuse, the Oise and Seine.

From Paris we follow the Marne to Epernay and Chalons en Champagne before returning to Landrecies for the Winter.

The following Spring we go south to Nancy and Toul before heading East on the Marne-Rhine canal to Strasbourg and thence to the mighty Rhine for a somewhat hairy two day passage to Mulhouse.

After that we travel the equally hairy River Doubs for our next wintering at St Symphorien.

The following year, after some expensive renewal work, we explore the central canals of France including the Nivernais before our next winter resting-place at Jo Parfitt's base in Laroche Migennes.

Our escapades include running aground, flooded bilges and a burglary, getting banned from driving, and held up for miles on end by obstinate bateliers.

I can tell your mouths are watering in anticipation.

Flow River Flow

The third book in the series about the voyages of Saul Trader on the waterways of Europe. Flow River Flow covers our travels on the Nivernais in France before a return to Holland for a repaint and a circular trip around the Netherlands before returning south via Belgium and the River Meuse to the Canal de L'Est and River Saone. Finally we bite the bullet and take the one-way street that is the mighty Rhone to the Camargue and Canal du Midi. Once again the book describes the characters that we encounter and attempts to describe the scenes with anecdote and humour. It is a social account of our travels rather than a detailed record of the history or the geography of the places we pass through. The primary object was to record the adventure with a touch of humour and a sprinkling of satire which I hope will put a smile on your face and even at times cause some laughter.

A Lot of Water Over the Bridge

This is the fourth and (probably) last in the Saul Trader series. We have now reached the sultry summer climes of the south of France and seem reluctant to return to the frozen north. We travel to the western end of the Midi encountering more characters in the shape of an enterprising Belgian hippie and his crazy Dutch girlfriend, a naval officer that goes by the name of Tommy Trinder and a boules-obsessed English country vicar. In the cosmopolitan city of Toulouse, a city of contrasts we find amongst the hubbub a real Irish bar and suffer once again at the hands of the kleptomaniac. There is solace on the Canal Garonne and an expensive and nearly disastrous repair job at Castets en Dorthe. Pretty towns come and go as we pass through the peaceful settlements of the Garonne - Moissac, Meilhan and Mas d'Agenais with its secret treasure. There are more characters, some good and some not so - a gift from the skipper of a hotel barge for being 'nice', a careless French mechanic who drives his van into my car, and Serge, a wonderfully helpful and proficient repairer of all things boat. We retrace steps back to the Rhone, crossing the large inland sea, the Étang de Thau, and are held up by more breakdowns resulting in parts having to be sent from England, and our guests bravely enduring 100° heat for hours on end to sort out problems with, of all things, overheating!

We finally return to the lovely welcoming port of Moissac where we find a permanent year-round mooring, something that we have never had before in the 20 years we have owned Saul Trader.

Reviews

Genuine

This is a joy to read and given the cliff edge ending I can't wait for volume three. Compulsive reading for those minded to venture to European waterways......Gareth

Bloomin' good read ..... Poshratz

Great chuckle - can't wait for the next book ..... could not put it down, read in one weekend laughed all the way through......
Barry

Loved reading and enjoyed it greatly. Quite informative. Look forward to your next book.
M Railey

The author gives us a wonderful travelogue, complete with background information, humorous anecdotes, and the occasional self-induced near-disaster. His viewpoint of a Brit on the mainland is very entertaining to those of us on the west side of the Atlantic.
W.D Silvestri

.... and maybe not !

'This chap hasn't a clue about barging. He doesn't crash into another boat in the entire book'...... T. West

'The best barge book I have ever read'.... ....Marjorie Tingwall, "Algebra for Beginners"

'Definitely not for the faint-hearted' ....A. Schwarzenegger

'or for the prudish'.........................Photo Editor, Health & Efficiency Magazine

'Humourous ! That's a laugh' ....*Anon*

'Very entertaining, great chuckle, can't wait for the next book'.......... *B Withers*

'I wish my dear husband had read this book years ago'........ ......*P.Scales (Mrs)*

'An absolutely superb masterpiece of literature - should become a classic'......*Keith Harris*

'You couldn't make it up'....................*Lars Björk, Technical Director, Ikea*

Printed in Great Britain
by Amazon

84540447R10119